PASSAGES

❀

Africa

PASSAGES

❧

AFRICA

❧

Contemporary Writing

from the Continent

PEN
AMERICA
free expression.
literature.

CONTENTS

FLASH

FABLE

POETRY

POETRY

MEMOIR

FICTION

PASSAGES

❧

Africa

The Tree of Life

MARTIN EGBLEWOGBE

First, it is important to visualise as far as is possible the street that runs in front of my house. I live in a quiet neighbourhood, home to a bunch of stuck-up bourgeoisie counting down their meaningless lives behind brick walls and hedges and lawns. Acacia, young and robust, line up beside the street, which sweeps out a gentle arc before stretching out to join the highway into the city, their leafy crowns casting shifting shadows on the light grey of the road.

Stepping out of my house one bright Saturday morning, I saw a man standing at the junction at the far end of the street. His arms were pressed to his sides, his gaze was fixed on some point far away, and he did not move. He looked decrepit and emaciated. I passed by without a word.

On my way back home he was still standing there. I went up to him.

"Is anything the matter?" I asked.

"It is here," he declared.

"What is here?"

"I have found it, at last, this spot. I've spent the whole of my life looking. At this very spot is the spiritual source that nourishes life."

"Very good," I said. "But you cannot stand here forever."

11

"Ah, but I can," he insisted, and there was no arguing with that.

He was still there the next morning.

"My dear friend," I said to him. "Will you not eat?"

"This is the source of life," he returned. "I need no more food."

In the evening he was still there. He seemed bigger and stronger, and looked well fed indeed. His voice was rich and resounding.

"You are looking good," I commented.

"Assuredly," he replied.

The days went by. I spoke to him whenever I passed and each time he had increased in stature. He had much to say, and I found his words wise and engaging. So it was that one day whilst thus engaged in conversation, a third person came up and asked me:

"My good man, why are you speaking to the tree?"

I replied without hesitation, "Here at this very spot is the spiritual force that nourishes life."

How African Spirits Were Born

RIBKA SIBHATU

TRANSLATED BY ANDRÉ NAFFIS-SAHELY

TRANSLATOR'S NOTE

Eritrean literature has been handed down through the generations in the form of *aulòs*, the Tigrinya term for bardic songs, which are performed at public and private celebrations as well as during religious rites. Performers always begin their tales by invoking the word *Şinşïwai*, which roughly means, "I have a story to tell," to which the audience replies *Uāddëkoi şęli-mai*, "We're ready, we're listening." Sibhatu learned her craft in Asmara and Hemberti, her ancestral village in the high plateau, where these stories can be traced back for centuries. "How African Spirits Were Born," the first fable presented in this selection, is popularly believed to be based on actual events and is thus performed without the usual introductory formula *Şinşïwai*. Eritrean tradition holds that spirits embody human forms and can be both malign and benign; for instance, the latter are thought to reside in pools of water, where people bathe in order to purify themselves and cure their illnesses. To this day, many claim to have seen spirits wandering through their homes or their villages, which explains why many are afraid to walk alone, especially at night, lest they fall victim to spirits less kindly inclined.

Once upon a time, there was a strong, wise emperor named Mersò, who ruled over the most powerful empire in Africa. When old age came knocking at his door, he summoned his firstborn son, who was his designated heir, and told him:

"Miren, my son, hear me. I have nourished my body long enough and now wish to make my peace with God and tend to my soul. The art of governing and the sense of responsibility it has imparted me tells me you are not suited to the wielding of power and that it would be best if your younger brother Gemel ruled in your stead."

"But this is absurd!" Miren exclaimed. "I'm your firstborn, how could you possibly crown him instead of me?"

His father replied, "Have you thought this through? And considered the consequences?"

"Yes!" his son answered. "If you don't honour my wishes, it'll mean there's no justice in this empire."

"So be it," his father concluded. "As such, I will divide the empire between you."

Emperor Mersò thus carved up the empire between his sons, and retired from public life to lead a hermit's existence. Far removed from royal pomp, he spent many years devoted to prayer and dined solely on herbs, roots, and wild berries: all in the quest to tend to his soul. However, Miren harboured great anger and resentment. Finally overwhelmed by it, he decided to kill his brother and thus be recognised as the sole, undisputed ruler of the empire! He paid Gemel a visit and told him:

"Brother!"

"Tell me," Gemel replied.

"I am the eldest!"

"Indeed you are . . . "

"As such, I should have inherited the entirety of the empire, but our father insisted on dividing it. However, it's time to rectify this: I want to kill you and seize all power for myself. Nevertheless, I don't ever want anyone to say I won it through subterfuge, and so prepare yourself for war. I'm coming for you."

Even though he now lived in the forest, the heavenly messengers warned the old emperor of what was about to happen in his lands. The emperor therefore decided to visit his sons. Once he'd arrived, he told them:

"My sons."

"Tell us," they said.

"What do you lack? Why are you fighting? I settled this matter before leaving you and now I've returned to broker peace!"

"I have no wish to settle!" Miren exclaimed. "Your solution meant there could never be peace! I should have been the sole ruler, but you forced me to share it with your son."

"Is that your final judgement?" his father asked.

"It is!"

"You wish to wield power alone?"

"I do!"

"Will you be able to handle it?"

"Of course, why wouldn't I? What does he have that I don't?"

"If that's the way you see it, then you must choose! Do you want to govern the visible world, or the invisible one?"

"If that's the way it has to be, then I choose the invisible world!"

Thus it came to pass. From that day forward, the emperor's eldest son and his followers became invisible: that's how African spirits were born, and ever since, they have fed on the food prepared by human beings.

xxv

CLIFTON GACHAGUA

the first flight of stairs goes into the room
with the operating table and trolley
—we've learnt to fuck on the unicycle, and the danger
of saying things for shock value—
the second disappears into a black nothing,
although i know there's a window there—
the air always cold, and the hum
of a thing caught in an Adam's grape.
the island in the kitchen is always dirty
from all the meals offered to strangers
who either arrive late, or come empty-handed.
old records used to be on the front wall,
now we have taarab and sounds no one will listen to.
the loop of these choruses, the madness
of stillness, incomplete fucks, books we will not read,
a broken appliance that might be turned
into a machine of love and time and friendship.
and in the private wing, an absence of light,
not the same as darkness—think of a child's body

the first time it experiences water, how instinct
cannot save it from drowning, instead,
enabling death. think of a great sinkhole.
backyard—more appliances, old shoes that
don't fit anymore, a dog licking milk from a condom,
flowers whose names we've forgotten, or
never cared to learn—like the way your body
moves in that awkward loop, until i turn you around, or
you turn me around, and we're finally nameless.
in the bin, a lecture on memory and the place
of the African writer in contemporary et cetera
—a thing we don't care about—your lucky beads,
the bangles from Z, bloody spit, bloody cotton,
and i think about the dog—do you think about the dog?

    he comes every day
for the milk and to lie down in the flowerbed,
to listen to the clock in the private wing.

xxvi

CLIFTON GACHAGUA

a)
if I'm to rely on memory, my country, you say,
is in the north—you are not sure.
(a woman cleans the rooms at the back,
her Swahili less labored than mine,
her answer to my imposition a nod of the head
and a return to duty, as if she's known
many more travelers like myself.
some music from somewhere dark, something
with its own rules and guides for memory-
making)
if I'm to rely on movement, the plastic flower
in my motel room
will remain a thing of beauty. &
I will stay here, with the dead TV,
the hood of a lamp, the half curtain,
the simple joys of the coming days,
—I'll make reliable lists from memory.
until you find me.
alone like this, with the body—

how also the map is torn in so many places
unwinding it is—or becomes—an act of grace—
something I'm incapable of.

b)

where does the body curve upwards, where down, where
does it say, or intend to say, this is hardness,
and this is the place you are not allowed to touch.

c)

if you don't know a thing to the absolute end of its meaning,
and let's assume there's a thing as that, the absoluteness,
like the texture of stone, the smell of sun in your unwashed hair—
does this count as memory?
like fucking in the dark, the difficulty of getting in,
which I hope has no meaning, and
the difficulty of rhythm   and pace,   even tone,
     and the lying
down afterwards, the closing of one pair of eyes and
the wandering in the dark of the other pair, head
tilted to where the window might be.

Normal

BREE

You are a lesbian contemplating life and future. He is purely hetero and thinks that lesbians are deviants. It is a shock to you the first time you have sex. Or perhaps you should say, the first time he fucks you, because that's what he does; with you bent over trying to disappear as he plunges into you, each thrust tearing into your identity that used to be certain. You know you should call it rape, but in some part of your head you enjoy it.

And that's what fucks you up. You enjoy it when he touches you; your breasts want his touch, your pussy moistens when he lies on your body; you spread your legs, you bend over, you kneel when he asks you to. And you enjoy it.

You never call the shots. You are not sure what the shots are. Head till morning? Reverse cowgirl? You didn't know these things before you discovered women.

You know his views about lesbians: they exist only to be watched . . . or fucked as a threesome. You have a couple. He watches as your fingers and mouth work the girl writhing under you. You smile at him. You cannot help the thought that this is all for him. He is sure that every lesbian just needs a dick, and when you dispute it, he points at you lying naked on the bed and says, But you're a lesbian, aren't you? He postulates about emotional trauma, mind orientation, religion, and unnaturalness . . . you try to change his mind, but he starts to change yours. You become the person in his head.

It's not all bad; you like him. In some part of your heart you love him. You know though that this is not the love that seizes your heart and sets it beating to a mad crazy tune. You are used to him; you understand him. You are grateful that he allows you to be bisexual. You start to think of life with a man. You lie on his chest and as you both doze off you decide that you can give up women.

The next time you are with a girl, it feels like the house you grew up in except all the doors have moved. You know what's inside but you have no clue how to get there. She smiles at you, you smile at her and you feel like a failure.

You start to push back against the woman he has in his head. You justify yourself—you talk to him about craving a wife. He asks you if this means you now want to be a man. You stop arguing. He tries to touch you and you fight him; it excites him so you stop. He takes you. You disappear as he pounds away. You feel him falter and then stop. You pick up your clothes and put them back on and try not to hate him or yourself.

One day he talks to you about the ones who tried to break you. He says, It was about control. You look at him, and the irony is a tart, bittersweet taste in your mouth. You realize this: he owns you until he decides that he no longer wants you. This is not about sexuality; this is about possession. You stop.

The next time he tells you all the different ways he is going to fuck you, you smile. You look for the excitement but it doesn't come. His mouth on your breasts does nothing. He fucks you with his fingers, trying to transfer the frenzy in his blood. You tell him that you are not wet; he says, You would be shocked at how wet you are. You don't explain that wet in your pussy is not the same as wet in your head.

He lays you down and starts to fuck you. You raise your legs to his waist and then over his shoulders. The pain hits with each stroke and when he sees your face he turns gentle, then stops, flips you over ass up—his favorite position. He plunges in and stops when you shriek. He lays you flat and starts again. You raise your ass obligingly, wind and moan . . . and when he tells you that he is about to cum, you tell him almost maternally to go ahead.

When he is done he asks, Why do I feel so stupid? You smile. For the first time since you started this, there is no anger or hate; there is no more confusion. You will stop justifying yourself to him. You will stop explaining what makes you a lesbian, stop trying to show him who you are. You will stop defining yourself by his normal.

The King of Buckingham Palace

ROTIMI BABATUNDE

At the beginning of the new school year, a student architect arrived in town saying he would be spending the whole year researching why a hilltop had been chosen as the best location for the old jailhouse. That the young man needed so long to determine such obvious reasons made some people start wondering if his intelligence was not less remarkable than that of a plodding donkey.

Everyone knew that the tenantless jailhouse had been built a century earlier for the monarch who challenged the pioneer colonial administrator to war. The battle that followed against the big guns of Europe was one the monarch's cheap muskets, doomed before the first shot had been fired, could never have won. The monarch's vanquishers thought a new home for the deposed potentate was necessary, and the old jailhouse on the hilltop was the outcome of that idea.

The ditch surrounding the hill served as a natural moat. After dropping a drawbridge over the ditch and erecting a fence with massive iron gates within its inner perimeter, the colonial authority had completed in little time a compound secure enough to quarantine their royal inmate but not forbidding enough to be called cruel. With a little fancy, the troublesome chap could even imagine himself as merely being away on a long, long tropical vacation, ha-ha, a colonial officer joked. All this was old knowledge, so no one saw sound reason in the trainee architect's mission to town.

The young man found nowhere more suitable for his lodgings than a room on the upper floor of Buckingham Palace, the rowdy brothel beside Central Market. The 33 girls of the house called him the Student and, without discrimination, he called each one of them My Dear. He often swore that when sober he could recite their proper names like his childhood catechism, but no one could confirm the claim since he was always drunk.

On his second day in town, the Student was seen standing by the stream, a good distance from the disintegrating drawbridge, staring with trepidation at the granite grimness that was the old jailhouse and the heavy wrought-iron gates that led into it.

Holy shit, the Student exclaimed. That was the closest he ever got to the premises. Afterwards, he burnt away his hours in the most seedy bars, strumming out highlife ballads from his guitar and arguing over rubbers with cardsharps at the gambling tables opposite the market entrance.

His favourite haunt was at the other end of the road from the card tables, the drinking den owned by the former priest who wore his collar all through his waking minutes despite having been excommunicated from the Church years ago. The place had no official name. Notwithstanding the stifling heat of its interior, it was known to all as the Mortuary, not because of the coldness of its drinks but because of the impressive body count from its frequent brawls.

❧

It was night, and in the Mortuary the Student was sitting by the counter. Disregarding the couples snuggling tighter in the bar's dark corners and the laughter rising along with cigarette and marijuana smoke from the crowded tables, the Student was busy downing bottle after bottle and plucking tunes on his guitar when the bloodiest violence witnessed at the place in recent memory erupted, sparked by an argument between the heads of two rival gangs over a girl.

The chairs in the bar flew like huge night birds through the dimness, and members of the opposing gangs began knocking the bottoms out of their bottles, transforming those bottles with familiar ease into jagged hand weapons. When the first gunshot went off, the sounds of doors and windows slamming shut in the neighbouring buildings followed. In the chaos of screaming and shouting, the Mortuary's patrons were now bailing out as if by prior agreement through every available exit. The battle also spilled out onto the streets. Hours passed before the gunfire dwindled to silence.

In his report, Inspector Salo, who led the first police squad to arrive at the Mortuary, would give details about the bodies they encountered on their way and the vehicles still burning on the streets and the grisliness of the bar that might well have been struck by a storm. He would note that the cops met only two living things that saw wisdom in remaining behind. One was the Student, who had just served himself a fresh bottle of beer and was sitting exactly where he had been before the brawl commenced. The young man was busy coaxing out another bawdy song from his guitar. The other was a white kitten crouching beside a pile of money on the counter, staring wide-eyed at the Student as if in disbelief.

❧

Inspector Salo should not have been shocked to see the Student sitting at the bar with such supreme tranquillity amidst that wreckage. Salo would later conclude that the devastation that had been wreaked on the

Mortuary could only have been an intimation of paradise to the Student, just like the slush on the roads must have been to the young man when he and the inspector first met. The world had been wet on that day of their initial encounter. It had been raining since the previous evening. The driver of Inspector Salo's squad vehicle joked that perhaps God was reneging on his promise not to wipe out creation with water again. The squad vehicle was heading down Market Road, which had become one slippery expanse of slush, when Inspector Salo and his men encountered the Student sitting in a pool of dirty water. Reeking like a brewery and unflustered by the relentless rain, the Student was drowning himself not only in the downpour but also in the nostalgia of hit songs from times past. The inspector regarded him with concern. Go home, Inspector Salo said.

I love you all, shouted the mud-splattered Student in reply.

Go home, Salo repeated. You have no business splashing around in that dirty water and singing in the freezing rain.

When did singing in the rain become a crime in this country, the Student asked.

Salo pondered over the question. The duties of the police did not include making sure drunks didn't catch a cold. No complaint had been lodged and the young man was not violent, so charging him with disturbing public peace would be overzealous. He gestured to his squad driver. The patrol van moved on.

The Student was still singing when a merry group of girls returning from choir practice stopped by. Men nearby stared at the dripping girls, captivated by the clinging of their wet clothes to the newly attained fullness of their bodies. Disregarding those ogling eyes, the girls wiped rainwater off their brows as they watched the singing drunk.

Hey, one of the girls said, don't you think you should be heading home now since it is cold and already getting dark?

The Student winked at the girls. He tried to get up but fell back on his buttocks, splashing muddy water as he slipped. The girls laughed.

Remember the wisdom of our elders, the Student said.

What?

A person who is beaten neither by the rain nor by the sun will be beaten dead by penury, the Student replied.

The girls skipped away, giggling at the drunk's debasement of the work ethic advocated by a venerable proverb. An hour later, the old barber with his shop nearby could no longer tolerate the singing. This is horrible enough to drive God crazy off His throne and fleeing with His angels for sanctuary in the very depths of hell, the old man said.

He went out into the rain to confront the Student. What sort of example are you trying to set, the barber asked. What will children think if they see you wallowing in the mud like a free-range pig and singing drunkenly as if you're the latest idiot in town?

The Student might have heard nothing. He continued singing. The barber, unacknowledged, returned grumbling to his shop.

The barber's shop was long shuttered and midnight was fast approaching when news of the Student's situation reached Buckingham Palace. Three ladies from the brothel came to take the young man home. With their assistance, he stumbled in the dark through the downpour, bawling out one filthy song after another. People peeped out of windows to watch the procession. The regular folk in their cosy homes shook their heads and wondered what the world was turning into, but the girls from Buckingham Palace didn't care and they found it all great fun as they helped the Student on.

The police van that had stopped earlier by the drunk was parked near the market's main gate. From its cabin, Inspector Salo regarded the approaching party. He heard the singing and recognised the voice. Salo's thoughts drifted to his son at home, an adorable darling who took his schoolwork seriously. The boy was always glad to run errands for aged folk. At the cathedral where he was a choirboy, the parishioners loved him and said he sang like an angel. His father had always been proud of him. Perhaps, once upon a time, the Student had also been a paragon among his peers, Salo thought. The inspector imagined his son in the Student's liquored circumstances, and he shuddered.

At the far end of the road, a car turned the corner. For a moment, the Student's mud-streaked face was caught in its headlights. He glared back at the lights, his eyes stoned and unapologetic. The inspector said nothing as the party passed. His expression was blank as he watched the three handlers assisting their charge up the steps of Buckingham Palace, but even after the party had disappeared into the building, Inspector Salo still felt unsettled by the fierceness he had seen burning like hell's embers in the Student's bloodshot eyes.

❧

So Salo shouldn't have been shocked when a few weeks later he encountered that same contrarian face in the deserted interior of the Mortuary, those same eyes gazing at the universe with unseeing defiance.

Have you gone mad, the inspector screamed.

The Student shrugged.

Didn't you hear the gunshots?

So?

Then why did you stay behind? What on earth are you still doing here?

Drinking my beer.

Bullets were flying all around . . . go outside, you'll see corpses . . . you could have been killed!

I have the right to drink my beer without interruption.

The finality with which the Student said that startled the inspector. He glanced around. The bar was in a shape even worse than he had assumed. His men were combing the premises for evidence. He turned back to the Student. This time the inspector's voice was gentler. You can't continue living your life like this, he said.

How?

Finish your studies. Get a good job. Marry a nice woman and settle down.

Why?

You will make good money. You will be able to buy the things you need.

The Student pointed at the kitten. There was a pile of money beside it. I have been paying for my beer, the Student said.

Beer is not what I am talking about, Salo said. There is nothing like living in a house of your own. You can build one and buy a nice car for yourself. Your family will live a good life. With time, you will become a top boss. Society will respect you. Your family will be proud of you.

The Student laughed.

I'm serious, Salo went on. Yes, there's some corruption in our country, but not everybody is a crook. You don't have to take bribes. You can influence how this country is run. Together, we can make the lot of mankind better. People will look up to you as a role model. In your old age, you will have wonderful stories to tell your grandchildren. When you look back on all the great things you have accomplished, you will feel happy and fulfilled.

Who told you I am not already happy and fulfilled, the Student asked. Why should I wait until I grow old to have what I'm enjoying now?

Salo had no response. What do you believe in, he asked after some seconds.

How?

Are you a Christian or a Muslim?

The Student pointed to the bottle of beer on the table. That's what I believe in, he said.

The inspector felt something strange happening to him. He didn't like how he was feeling.

The Student continued talking. We will all be dead sooner or later, he said. Even the sun and all the stars will get dark and cold. Time itself will become one long unending night. No memory will remain of anything which ever existed.

Salo looked away, feeling empty inside. It seemed the foundation of his world was disintegrating under his feet and that he was tumbling headlong into the nothingness it was leaving behind.

The Student resumed drinking. The other cops had been observing the interlocutors from a distance, wondering what their superior found worthwhile to discuss with a drunk. One of them walked up to the inspector.

Oga, we suppose arrest this man, the policeman said.

The inspector shook his head.

But, sir . . . na him be the only witness we meet for here.

Let him be, Salo snapped. He couldn't explain why he was so disoriented. Nausea began welling up in his guts. Perhaps it was the dank oppressiveness of the Mortuary that was suffocating him. Salo walked out of the bar. In the open air, he still didn't feel any better.

When Salo returned home, he told his wife that what shocked him the most was not that the trainee architect would have remained unmoved if the universe was in the process of being annihilated, or even that the young man did not flinch when he learnt about the bartender whose bloody corpse the inspector and his men had seen being licked near the bar's entrance by a pack of homeless dogs. All that was trumped by the lunatic drama Salo observed going on between the Student and the kitten. In the course of the night's apocalyptic events, the Student had been lodging payment for the beers he had been serving himself with the white kitten, which he reckoned a fit and proper financial representative of its owner, the excommunicated priest.

In his report to his superiors, the inspector would recommend that the Mortuary be shut for good and the Student be given psychiatric help. His counsel would not be heeded. Less than a fortnight later, following the bar proprietor's visit to the home of the police chief clutching a heavy briefcase, the establishment was buzzing once more with the crush of swinging patrons and the Student was back at his favourite spot by the counter, drinking beer with the persistence of a dehydrated camel and strumming his guitar with consummate abandon.

❧

Friday nights were the busiest at the Mortuary. For the mechanics and hairdressers and bus conductors and other blue-collar workers who thronged the place, participating in those Friday night festivities was sufficient vindication for the previous week of backbreaking work, their own midnight Sabbath consecrated to the joys of drunken revelry.

The Student always joined the proceedings early on Friday evenings and never left until long after the sun was up on Saturday. On one such Saturday, amidst the cigarette butts and used condoms and the other assorted detritus of the previous night's saturnalia, the Mortuary's gardener discovered the Student cradling his guitar like a lover and snoring serenely in a pool of his own puke.

All attempts to rouse the Student, even with a baptism of icy water, were futile, so the gardener continued his tasks. The only green thing in the premises was the algae growing on the drainpipes, and that irony was not lost on other staff members of the Mortuary, some of whom kept teasing the gardener by asking him if his day's harvest of condoms was good. Unfazed, the gardener went about his work, which was limited to gathering trash.

His chores that Saturday were not completed until noon. Afterwards, he stopped to pick up his wages at the proprietor's office. The office was lined with shelves of leather-bound texts, almost all with Latin and Greek titles scripted in medieval calligraphy. The excommunicated priest was seated behind his desk, dressed in a tuxedo and sporting his ever-present clerical collar.

I don ready to go, sir, the gardener said.

The proprietor looked up from a dog-eared copy of Origen's Septuagint beside the diminishing bottle of whisky on his desk. Have you finished clearing all yesternight's junk from the bar, the proprietor asked.

Yes, sir.

The proprietor shook his head in disagreement. But on my way up here I saw the Student still snoring on the floor, he said.

I don try wake am, sir, the gardener replied. The Student . . . him condition no different from that of Lazarus. I swear, na only God fit resurrect am.

Ah, that is where you are missing the point. There is no need to wake him. Or do you waste your time trying to wake up the garbage before taking it to the dump?

The gardener was perplexed. No, not at all, he slowly replied.

The bar owner took a swig of whisky from the bottle. Then he asked, Where, as the saying goes, does garbage have its residence?

The refuse hill na garbage house. Na so the proverb talk.

And in your work here, with what do you carry garbage to its residence?

The wheelbarrow wey you buy for me, sir.

Correct! So, as everyone knows, where does the Student have his residence?

Buckingham Palace. Na Buckingham Palace the man dey stay, the gardener said, his eyes lighting up with understanding.

Good, the proprietor said, nodding. He turned his attention back to the antique Bible on his desk. When you have completed today's cleaning, return here to collect your wages, he concluded.

The gardener's wheelbarrow was the sturdiest available in stores. His fellow workers assisted in lifting the drunken fellow onto its tray. There was no problem with the guitar because even in his slumber the Student held it in a tight embrace, and though the Student's legs were dangling over the tray's rim, his toes had sufficient clearance from the ground.

The route to Buckingham Palace went mostly downhill, so the gardener's task was light. He whistled a tune to himself as he pushed. At the time the gardener and the Student exited the Mortuary's gate, their only fellow travellers had been the houseflies buzzing around the yellow puke caked around the Student's mouth, but within minutes, there were already several children jumping up and down in the gardener's wake, the little ones intrigued by the absurdity of an adult being trundled home. The children improvised a new song, chorusing it as they ran after the wheelbarrow.

> *The King of Buckingham Palace*
> *The snoring King of Buckingham Palace*
> *All hail Mr Wheelbarrow*
> *The drunken King of Buckingham Palace*

On arriving at Central Market, people ceased trading and strained their necks to catch a view of the passing procession, the women gasping in empathy when the wheelbarrow lurched into a pothole and it seemed the Student would be flung into the ditch. By the time the gardener turned onto the final stretch leading to Buckingham Palace, the retinue of clapping and singing children had reached carnival numbers, as if the Student were a latter-day Pied Piper serenading them towards debauchery at the brothel with diabolic music from his mute guitar.

❧

That incident marked the Student's ascension to the throne. The girls in the brothel held a raucous party to celebrate his coronation as the

King of Buckingham Palace, and all around town people began address-
ing the new potentate as appropriate. Long live the King, they greeted
whenever they encountered him.

Just a month into the reign of the Student, his kingship was thrown
into crisis by rebellion from within his palace. Weeks would pass before
Inspector Salo stumbled upon information about that insurrection. He
was sitting on a bench under the mango tree in front of the police station when the squad driver, who had been busy leafing through a glossy
magazine, let out a whoop. Salo gave the driver a quizzical look.

Isn't she lucky, the squad driver said, pushing the magazine in Salo's
direction. He pointed out a picture to the inspector. The photograph,
taken at a party graced by top socialites, was of a young lady and a
wrinkled old man.

Who are they, Salo asked.

That's the girl from Buckingham Palace . . . the one that took on the
Student!

Inspector Salo frowned. After his conversation with the Student at the
Mortuary, Salo had lost interest in reading bedtime stories to his son,
and he stopped bringing biscuits home. It is the stress of Daddy's work
that makes him forget, Salo's wife consoled the boy. But she became wor-
ried when her husband discontinued plastering her with playful kisses
and bellowed at her whenever she asked him what was bothering him.
Then he ceased going to church, and she began wondering if a lookalike
intruder had not replaced him on their matrimonial bed.

The inspector's troubles were also noticed at his workplace. The
trademark smartness of Salo's uniform became a thing of the past, and
he began arriving late to work. Not that his superiors minded. Most
of them considered his previous scrupulousness an indictment of their
shortcomings. The members of his squad were even more pleased. Salo
was no longer an impediment to extortion and bribe collection, and they
all thanked God for their inspector's new incarnation, except for the
squad driver, who missed the old Salo. The inspector had encountered

all kinds of people in the course of his work, but the Student was a different proposition. To prevent his life being thrown into further chaos, he had adjusted his patrol routes to avoid running into the Student. He wasn't eager to hear about any matter connected with the Student.

I am happy for the girl, the driver said, startling Salo out of his thoughts. The lucky girl has hit the jackpot!

Well, I'm not interested, Salo said, but the driver began telling Salo about the revolt against the King of Buckingham Palace. Several weeks earlier, the young man had paid his daily visit to the gaming tables. He was baffled when the table owners refused to deal for him. We don't want any trouble from the police, they said.

It took a while before the Student learnt that one of the 33 girls in Buckingham Palace was interested in his whereabouts. He owed the girl money for a night of pleasure, and she had come around hunting for him with a carving knife.

But I will surely pay her when I have the money, the Student protested. That I drink a lot does not mean I'm not honourable.

The table owners laughed and started spinning wisecracks about young men who consider themselves holier than Angel Michael despite fucking prostitutes on credit. Unable to endure their riling, the Student huffed away from the card tables.

On reaching the Mortuary, he was further frustrated when the waiters refused to take his order. A girl from Buckingham Palace came here asking for you, the headwaiter said.

How is that any of your business?

It appears the girl came from a good Christian home. Do you know what she said when she came here?

I'm dying of thirst, the student shouted. Just serve me a beer! I haven't been this sober since the day I came bawling out of my mother's womb.

Behold, the wages of the labourers who mowed your fields, which you kept back by fraud, are crying out against you, the headwaiter said. That was the verse from the Holy Book the girl quoted. She must have been attentive in Sunday school!

Ask her when she last read any book at all, holy or not. I will pay the girl her money soon. I always clear my bills once I get money.

I believe you, my good friend. But if anything happens here, the police will disturb us, not the girl.

I will report her to the police if she doesn't stop this nonsense.

The Student's threat made the headwaiter laugh so hard he had to wipe away his tears. Young man, the headwaiter said, the police have more serious things to do than resolving disagreements between prostitutes and their customers. The same girl stabbed someone here two years ago and nothing happened. It took us days to scrub all the blood off the carpet.

Wait . . . wait a moment . . . is what you are telling me . . . is it really the truth, the Student asked, his eyes widening with anxiety.

The waiter pointed at the cigarette-burnt settee in a corner of the bar. Right there, he said. The man was dead before he got to the hospital. Nothing happened to the girl, but my boss had to pay the police a hefty bribe.

That is not possible, the Student said, but with his throat now dry and his voice drained of conviction.

So we don't want that kind of trouble here again. You must leave.

You can't be serious, the Student replied. Listen, I buy drinks here every day and you think you can just drive me out like a . . .

Mindful of his own safety, the headwaiter had jumped away from the Student before shouting, Hey! Watch! She's back!

The waiter was pointing at the bar's entrance, towards which the girl who had asked after the Student was now heading. The Student turned and saw the butcher's knife glinting in his creditor's hand. He screamed.

Later, his most ardent fans would argue that if the great King of

Buckingham Palace had had enough alcohol in his system, he would merely have put down that insurrection against his throne with his customary indifference, but the Student's detractors would insist that it was the nightmarish vision of his entrails eviscerated on the bar's floor that jolted the King of Buckingham Palace out of his alcoholic haze and spurred him into instant motion. Unlike the incarcerated monarch for whom the jailhouse had been constructed, the Student shunned the perilous allures of valour and opted instead for flight. As if propelled not by his own volition but by an implacable force against which he was helpless, the Student was already hurtling through the bar's back door when the brothel girl made her entrance. Still, the beer bottle she hurled towards his fleeing figure missed his ear only by the closest inch.

The deposed King of Buckingham Palace realised there was no better destination for him than the nearest motor park. By the time the brothel girl tailed him to the park, the bus he had boarded was already in motion, taking him away at top speed from the town and from the old jailhouse inside which he never once stepped.

At the park, while taking a drink to console herself, the girl from Buckingham Palace was chatted up by a rich trader from out of town who knew nothing about her occupation. That trader was the same doddering baldhead beside whom she would be pictured some weeks later in the magazine Salo's squad driver was leafing through under the mango tree in front of the police station.

What a lucky girl, the squad driver exclaimed.

You call that luck?

The girl relocated from town to move in with the trader only a few days after they met, the driver said. That he took her to such a glamorous party means he is serious with her. People are happy for the girl. They say the trader plans to marry her soon in a lavish church ceremony. She couldn't have gotten a better return on the debt owed her by the Student, could she?

The inspector looked again at the picture of the Buckingham Palace girl and her aged partner. It seemed to him that the girl looked somewhat sad. The inspector imagined the pampered boredom of the girl's new existence as housewife to a vulture-bald trader.

That man is old enough to be the girl's grandfather, Salo said. Marriage to a toothless rich man doesn't seem like paradise to me. I don't see how her new station in life is any less horrible than the previous.

What if they love each other, the squad driver asked. Who then are we to pass judgement on them?

Salo shrugged. The two men said nothing for a while. The silence was broken by the inspector. The girl is gone, Salo said. That means the Student will return.

No, the driver replied.

Truly?

The girl's carving knife has terrified the Student so much that he has sworn never to set foot in this town again.

Salo felt a weight lifting off him. He rose. Thank you, he said. Thank you so much for that information.

The inspector began walking away. The driver watched him go, baffled by Salo's effusive gratitude, then he returned his attention to the magazine.

❦

That evening, Salo arrived home early. His wife noticed her husband's old gaiety beaming out of his face again. Salo winked at her and kissed her on the forehead. She looked at him with surprise. He hadn't done that in a long time. Their son was busy with his homework in a corner. The woman watched her husband walk up to hug the boy, then Salo gave him the biscuits he had bought on his way home.

You're happy today, the woman said. What happened?

The Student is gone, Salo replied. On Sunday, we must give thanks for that in church.

Salo's wife continued marvelling at the miracle of her husband's transfiguration. The gloom that had settled upon him since his encounter with the Student at the Mortuary had lifted. What greater confirmation of that miracle could she have wished for than seeing him back by her side in church, dancing once more around the altar and singing songs of praise to the heavens without vacillating? Already, she could see the two of them and their son departing church after service, heading home together for Sunday lunch like any regular family, and she smiled because that was what she and her husband had always desired.

How to Eat a Forest:
In Two Acts

BILLY KAHORA

ACT 1: CARTOGRAPHIC PATA POTEA

Almost everywhere, the redefinition of internal boundaries was carried out under cover of creating new administrative districts, provinces, and municipalities. These administrative divisions had both political and economic goals.

> — *Achille Mbembe*
> *"At the Edge of the World:*
> *Boundaries, Territoriality, and Sovereignty"*

Sometime in the late 1990s, a small number of individuals from the south of Narok District, Maasailand, holding title deeds, started making regular trips west and northwest into neighbouring Kalenjin land. The land brokers from Maasailand left their vast, cow-dung streaked and undisturbed plains and deep indigenous forests and travelled to the highly populated highlands of Bomet and beyond, as far as Nyamira District, Kisii. There they found large families, of three generations and even four, cramped onto as little as half an acre of land–working land that had been tilled season after season and was now choking.

In the west the land brokers found land-hungry Kipsigis, Kisii, and Luhya people who were mostly teachers, small-scale farmers, small businessmen and shopkeepers looking for land. But the visitors from Maasailand, who were actually selling a bountiful future, were a curious medley, the kind of disparate mishmash of fortune seekers found on any frontier that is up for grabs. They came in all sizes and packages: land brokers from the dusty streets of Narok town; agents affiliated to crooked Narok County councillors; sidekicks of powerful local provincial administration figures; members of a powerful political Narok family; Kalenjin individuals connected to Kalenjin MPs with access to new land deals; and the odd Ogiek individual.

All that the land brokers had in common was that they were vigilantes of acreage and *mpaka* (border). The frontier in question was the southern part of the Mau Forest Complex, also known as Mau South (the Maasai call it the Maasai Mau, a name heavily disputed by the Ogiek, who claim to be indigenous forest dwellers occupying the forests that lie adjacent to Masaai plains). This frontier was a boon to those living in the once fertile, but now overpopulated, volcanic Kalenjin land and the Kisii highlands.

These travellers of fortune went among the Kalenjin and Kisii small landholders and told amazing tales of *kitiya*, land that is untilled and virgin and up for sale, cheap. They promised tens of bags of harvest from a single acre. They scouted for potential buyers in the bars, tea and *mandazi* cafes of small trading centres. The names of these places would soon be replicated in their new Narok District homes, when the immigrants settled, and Narok soon acquired a Nyamira Ndogo, a Chebalungu Ndogo and a Kericho Ndogo. There was even a place called Sierra Leone, named after the peacekeeping soldiers from West Africa who came back from that conflict and bought land in the area with their severance pay. Many of the immigrants actually held real title deeds produced from the dusty corridors of the Narok Ministry of Lands office, and sales agreements drawn up by crooked Narok town lawyers. The land brokers promised protection; the land they were offering belonged to the *mkubwa* (big men) from Narok South who also had friends in government. And so evolved one of the largest land grabs in Kenyan history.

The premise was simple and devastating: the crooked lawyers and surveyors arbitrarily changed the representation on a map to a magnification that stretched into the nearby Mau South Forest, a "neutral" and vast territory that was a natural space of forest that no one was protecting or looking after—or rather, had no private ownership of, the Mau South Forest protected by the Narok County council. Beyond the Narok border, the Mau Forest on Kalenjin land was protected by the government, as gazetted by the Kenyan parliament. There the forest remained sacrosanct and untouched. So lands that bordered the Mau South forest stretched for miles inside and all around the edges of the Mau within the Narok boundaries. Small parcels of land multiplied into their tens as land surveyors were instructed to redraw the map of the original piece of land and eat up the forest.

There were several other schemes. At times land was sold by the agent/broker to a relatively poor immigrant, and subsequently offered by the politically connected seller to a prominent national government official. This was in exchange for political patronage. The gamble was that although the immigrant would soon occupy the land, the prominent national politician would hardly bother to actually visit the piece of land, let alone take real ownership. One piece of land could thus be used for both financial gain and political reward. Also, in the overtures and initial negotiations in Kisii and Bomet, promises were made and cash deposits given by the land-hungry as a commitment of interest. Once the preliminary agreement was signed, a date was set for the new landowners to come to Narok to finalise the deal. Sometimes these deals never panned out, and many lost their deposits to crooked brokers. The clearing of the forest also generated timber and charcoal for the sellers. The new areas brought in retail commerce that was controlled by cartels connected to the sale of the forest. A thriving new economy was created in all sorts of ways.

So, acre by acre the Mau South forest was illegally sold. The architects behind the illegal sale of the Maasai Mau were later said to be shocked at the extent of what they had started. Once the concept of an undefined *mpaka* filtered into the Narok countryside's psyche and became the norm, it dawned upon the culprits that the forest they had started selling was not limitless and the tide was almost unstoppable. By then it was too late. Thousands of hectares of the Mau South had been sequestered. And the forest had been almost completely eaten.

What eventually stopped the game was the change of political regimes in December 2002, when Mwai Kibaki took over from Daniel arap Moi. And so the language of eating forest completely changed. Suddenly all the land-buying immigrants were labelled encroachers (the majority were from Moi's tribe, the Kalenjin, who found themselves at a disadvantage within the new political dispensation), even if they had possibly given up their life savings for virgin land with real title deeds. "Encroaching" became the new buzz word. The fashionable word in independent Africa has always been "squatter" in this kind of circumstance. But an encroacher was seen as a "foreign invader", whereas a squatter was a property-less local individual. A squatter was considered to be relatively harmless, while the encroacher was seen to be intruding upon and seizing property that had been clearly mapped and was already owned. In the Mau context, a primordial hatred developed towards encroachers.

This distinction was a signifier of how completely things had changed in the Mau scenario after a change of government. Whereas the older immigration had been part of a larger "deal" in which all involved benefitted, "encroaching" became part of a new and larger political game. At the heart of the game was a misrepresentation of epic proportions, and now these so-called encroachers were seen as Kalenjin agents planning to completely recreate a political boundary that encroached into Maasailand by pushing the Bomet district boundary into Narok district. The game was redefined as a classic case of changing internal administrative boundaries and maps to the advantage of the ruling regime. The accusation was one of gerrymandering.

Hand-in-hand with this debate about who was an encroacher and who was "genuine" was another aspect of the Mau South issue—the question of indigeneity. Among the title deed brigade from Narok District involved in the illegal sale of the forest were individuals from the Narok Ogiek community. The Ogiek seemed to have emerged into the national psyche around 1994, after the United Nations declared an International Day for Indigenous People. Non-governmental organisations were set up in Narok by individuals, until then popularly known as Ndorobos, to start fighting for their rights. The leaders of this movement took up their new name, the Ogiek (meaning "caretaker of all animals and plants") and claimed a unique and conservation-friendly relationship with the forest.

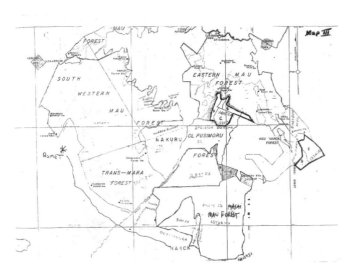

Map created by Graeme Arendse

ACT 2: PRACTISING FOREST, SELLING SHAMBAS

Most of these conflicts are expressed in the form of an opposition
between autochthonous populations and strangers. Citizenship
is conceived in ethnic and territorial terms, and an individual's
enjoyment of civil rights depends on his appurtenance to an eth-
nic group or locality.

> — *Achille Mbembe*
> *"At the Edge of the World:*
> *Boundaries, Territoriality, and Sovereignty"*

Travelling along the recently built Narok-Kisii Highway back in 2005, at
the height of the Mau South saga, the road is an arrow-straight, mirror-like
asphalt running parallel to the rapidly shrinking southernmost borders of
the Mau South Forest. Feeder roads turn to the right and branch in the
general direction of the forest every 15 km. The land is flat and monoto-
nous, and even in a speeding car one feels as if standing still. A truck in the
distance looks like a Matchbox toy. The horizon is so straight that the edge
of the sky looks like a brilliant fairy tale lake from Hans Christian Ander-
sen. We feel as if we are at the end of Kenya, and in a sense we are. The
southernmost border of Narok District is also the Tanzania-Kenya border.
The Mau South Forest starts 17 km from Narok town. It has an area of
46,278 ha and sits astride Narok District, extending west and north. It is
the southernmost part of the once 290,000 ha Mau complex that borders
Kericho to the west and Nakuru to the north. It is often said that it was
once larger than Nairobi Province.

We are looking for an Ogiek man, Samuel Kamikil, who, we are told, knows how the forest was eaten. We go down the first road off the Narok Highway that turns off in the general direction of the Maasai Mau Forest into Ngareta location. The Ogiek, according to some, have lived here for at least three generations. Ngareta location straddles both north and south Narok and is about 20 km from Narok town. Further down the highway there are three more right turns that lead into other small Maasai, Kipsigis, and Ogiek communities and trading centres—Chebulenga, Ololonga and Mulot—and eventually into the forest. The first and third names respectively are Luyha and Kalenjin—signs of the modern colonisation that took place in these spaces in the late 1990s and into the millennium. Some of the roads leading to the forest's southern border were built for the sole purpose of illegally accessing the forest.

The straight, dusty road we travel on to meet this man, Kamikil, is of the kind that grinds the bones and the drive shafts of a car. We meet combine harvesters, tractors, black mamba bicycles, and an old drunken woman who flags us down and proceeds to curse heavily when we stop. She then makes out as if to spit, but all that comes out is the harsh question "*Mnataka msitu*?" You want forest?

We find Samuel Kamikil sitting by the roadside with his children. The Ogiek say that they recognise each other from looking at the eyes. Our first impression of Kamikil is his weird and close resemblance to the U.S. actor Scott Glenn. Kamikil is tough, sharp-eyed, wiry, thin, and outdoorsy but at the same time extremely soft-spoken and self-deprecating. He has riveting, piercing eyes like the actor.

As we start our interview the motors of illegal chainsaws deep in the forest stir the quiet air. This is just several hours after meeting officials from the Narok District headquarters who told us that everyone had been evicted from the forest. On our way to meet Kamikil we frequently edged towards the margins of the narrow road to let Canter after Canter pass by. The load at the back was usually completely covered with tarpaulin, but our guide told us that the vehicles were probably ferrying timber or charcoal to Nakuru. There, a well-connected Nakuru timber miller was making millions.

Samuel Kamikil does not remember the exact year he was born. "*Nilizaliwa wakati wa Mau Mau. Siku Hio.* I was born at the time of the Mau Mau." Those days. He suddenly hands over his ID, and it gives his date of birth as 1964, at least six years after the Mau Mau surrendered. Also, the name on his ID is Salaton Ole Nadunguenkop, which is a Maasai name unlike most Narok Ogiek names. Ogiek names are actually Kalenjin. And Kamikil sounds like a Kalenjin name—we have yet to figure out why he has two names. The Ogiek claim that the taking of Maasai or Kalenjin names happened back in 1930 when a colonial proposition to the Land Commission to assimilate the Ogiek into the neighbouring tribes with whom they had closest affinity was enforced.

On the side of the road, Kamikil remembers an idyllic childhood gathering honey and hunting game. Life was dictated by the migration cycles of bee colonies. "*Kila Ndorobo alikuwa anaishi kwa mlima yake.* The community I was born in consisted of about 500 individuals and we had our own hill. Our life was of many kilometres. The bees always led us to the honey. Land did not belong to anyone. We went where the bees went. The worst thing that could happen was the disappearing of the flowers that the bees liked. We were then forced to live on meat," Kamikil recalls.

We say nothing of the fact that Kamikil uses the name "Ndorobo" unproblematically. Most of the Ogiek we have met so far have discarded the un-PC "Ndorobo" for "Ogiek". "*Il Ntorobo*" means "poor" in Maasai. He then tells us how his community started farming in the early 1970s, when he was still a child. This was because of exposure to other foods outside the forest world. He remembers that that was when other aspects of "Ndorobo" life started changing.

"Before we started building huts we were living in *ngabuna* (structures of leaf, branches, and bark). We also lived inside stony hillsides where we spent nights and rainy days.

"*Hakuna chief. Kulikuwa na wazee wakusema wasipite mlima ile kwenda kuchukua asali ya wale wengine. Usivuke mpaka. Ile mzinga iko pande hiyo ni ya nani.* There was no chief. There were just elders that controlled the hills and the honey. *Hatukuwa tunaona watu wengine. Tulikuwa tunapelekea watu asali ya kutairisha watu na kuolewa.* We were the only ones in the world. Honey was our money. That's what we used to get circumcised and as dowry."

He talks of an idyllic time when Ogiek clans lived in harmony and migrated to and fro within the Mau Forest. Then, he says, he became lucky. His father insisted on his attending school and that was when he obtained an ID and he became known to the Republic of Kenya as Salaton Ole Nadunguenkop. But he still kept his identity as Samuel Kamikil from his childhood.

Suddenly the old Maasai woman we met on the roadside on the way to the interview appears. She has a friend in tow and they start shouting drunkenly from the road at us sitting in the grass. All I can make out is "*Ndorobo, Ndorobo*". This goes on for several minutes and then they move on, muttering loudly. One of the other Ogiek men sitting with us tells us the woman was accusing Ndorobos of selling the forest. He laughs nervously. We learn later that this is the general sentiment in Narok District among the Masaai when it comes to the Ogiek. Many Maasai, including a Narok County councillor we talk to, hold the "Ndorobo" in the lowest possible regard. Statements about the Ogiek are either dismissive or extremely bigoted. The councillor tells us that the Maasai have never disturbed the forest, which was used as a grazing area during drought in the lower plains south of the Mau South Forest.

Kamikil promises to take us into the forest the next day to show us his home that was burned and destroyed by the National Alliance of Rainbow Coalition (NARC) government. Curiously, he does not talk of the Kenyan police or the Narok provincial administration. I ask him whether I should call him by his Ogiek name, Samuel Kamikil, or the one recognised by the Republic of Kenya, Salaton Ole Nadunguenkop. He pauses, then grins. "*Unaweza Niita Salaton*. Call me Salaton."

Before we drive off he insists we take a photo of him in traditional skins. It is important for the world to know how the Ogiek live. He is dressed like any modestly prosperous Kenyan farmer: nondescript canvas jacket, collared flowered shirt, standard khaki trousers and safari boots, complete with a cane. His son, a boy in his early teens, has been fiddling with my cellphone and asks me to bring him one like it the following day.

The next day we meet Kamikil and bring a guide called Michael Setek with us. Setek is the treasurer of a local NGO known as Friends of the Mau Forest. He is also Maasai and has lived in the area all his life, and has been fighting for the protection of the Mau South Forest since he was in his teens. When we try to introduce Setek to Ole Nadunguenkop, the former laughs loudly. The two exchange a greeting that we've never heard. "B-o-p" is roughly what it sounds like. Ole Nadunguenkop gives a wry grin. We drive to the edge of the Mau South forest and start to walk into it in single file. We are at the extreme boundary of Narok South constituency and once we cross the river into the forest we enter into Narok North. We leave MP Ole Ntutu's land and enter MP Ntimama's country, which is still dense, undisturbed forest.

Setek and I walk slightly ahead. A colleague walks behind us with the man we are now thinking of as Salaton Ole Nadunguenkop, as constantly reaffirmed by Setek. Often Ole Nadunguenkop shouts directions from behind when we come to forked paths. Once we are in the forest, Ole Nadunguenkop exudes a calm authority, unlike yesterday's measured deference. We move from sparse tree cover to a large flat glade and start climbing into deep, thick forest. The air becomes fresher as we reach higher altitudes. Though it is a relatively hot day, it is wet and cool in the forest. Setek laughs when I enquire how he knows Kamikil.

"*Huyu mtu mnaita Kamikil na mjua sana. Ameuza msitu sana.* This man you are calling Kamikil I know him very well. He is Ole Nadunguenkop. He has sold a lot of the forest.

"*Huko Ngareta anashamba kubwa. Hakuna shida yuko nayo. Anaishi kwa mama yake. Huu mtu anapeleka mpaka Subaru. Ya brown.* In Ngareta he has a large *shamba*. Or his mother has a large *shamba* that was once part of the group ranch that was given to the Ogiek, then later subdivided. He is not destitute. He even has a car. A Subaru. A brown one.

"*Hii maneno ya Mau ni kali sana. Utapata watu wanakuambia maneno ya uwongo. Hata ile maneno mimi nakuambia lazima udoublecheck.* This Mau thing is very complex. People will be telling you lies and all sorts of things. Even for me you must double-check everything I tell you."

I listen to this as I am still trying to digest the information about Kamikil and his car. Setek speaks a Maasai Swahili expressed entirely in the third person, and it is at times hard to decipher what he is saying. I think back to the previous day. At the end of our conversation with Kamikil, we had been sufficiently moved by his measured tales of woe with the NARC government to give his sons several hundred shillings, after listening to his family's account of homelessness and destitution following the evictions.

My Nairobi sense of the hustle has perked up, and on hearing Setek's story, I now look at Ole Nadunguenkop with less pity and more respect. Part of me sees him as a man of enterprise. I even stop asking him when we will come across one of his beehives. And though the claim that his family (Kamikil) has been rendered landless is now dubious, we will learn later that there are 30 Ogiek families who were evicted in spite of possessing genuine title deeds, and are now living in Nakuru with relatives.

Suddenly we hear noises in the shrubbery. A man carrying a large wooden post on his shoulder appears. He looks alarmed and sheepish when he sees us. We partly expect him to flee. Ole Nadunguenkop soon catches up with us and the man loses all discomfiture. Ole Nadunguenkop exchanges rapid words in Kipsigis with the post-bearing individual.

"*Unapeleka hiyo post wapi?*" Setek then asks. Where are you taking that post?

"*Hii post ni ya huyu,*" the man says quickly. He points at Ole Nadunguenkop. This post belongs to him. With nothing else to say, the man quickly passes us and continues hurtling down the hill. There are birds all around us, and the stream that serves as the border between Narok North and Narok South constituencies gurgles nearby. A ray of sunlight lands on Ole Nadunguenkop's head through the leafy canopy above.

As we climb higher there are more trees now, and it is ever more silent. Now and then we find a felled tree and several posts lying around it. We go through dense underbrush for about 20 minutes and suddenly come into a clearing straight out of the TV version of Swiss Family Robinson. There is a clearly demarcated homestead with three wooden huts, two mud ones and a small goat shed. Sloping around the buildings is some of the finest crop of maize we have ever seen. But weeds are now growing through it. There are also fat cabbages and sprouting beans. All around the clearing are tall, dense trees. This is Ole Nadunguenkop's home. I can't imagine how the new NARC government ever found him. Later we will learn there are homesteads still deeper in the forest.

As we stand there silently, the post-bearing man suddenly reappears from the trees. He tells us his name, and that he originally hails from beyond Bomet town and is Kipsigis. He came to Narok a year ago and Ole Nadunguenkop "sold" him a piece of land. There were no title deeds in this particular transaction, and it took place in a different time before NARC would ever have found Ole Nadunguenkop.

"*Ukikuja unaongea tuu na Mzee (Ole Nadunguenkop),*" the man says. One would just talk to Ole Nadunguenkop. The man eventually married into his new benefactor's family and occupies the homestead next to Ole

Nadunguenkop. He farms his own land and also doubles as a worker for the "old man," Ole Nadunguenkop, now and then when needed. Cutting down the odd tree. There is a pile of fresh-looking posts next to the burnt shell of Ole Nadunguenkop's former home. In Kiambu the small pile would be worth several thousand shillings.

Today things have become very different very quickly, triggered by a series of coincidences—the most important of which is inadvertently having brought Setek along with us. Yesterday Samuel Kamkil was extremely voluble about his life as an Ogiek. Today, as Ole Nadunguen-kop, he seems uneasy. He admits to us that he has no title deed for this particular piece of land. But he says this as if it is of no consequence, and without any irony. Like a man talking about the weather. At the heart of it, he is Samuel Kamikil, an Ogiek, and believes that the forest belongs to him and he can sell it as he wills.

When we ask who else has sold land in the forest, Ole Nadunguenkop says he and his brother have a land association. He is the chairman. "Inaitwa Ogiek Association Group," he says. This is the first time since we've met him that he has used the term "Ogiek." I do not ask whether the association is registered.

Ole Nadunguenkop does not say much when we eventually leave. There is no further talk of photos in traditional skins. There is no more talk of honey and showing us his beehives. We leave him to live his oddly double life. Later, he sends a mistaken message of gratitude to us through Setek after the new NARC government eventually promises the Ogiek title deeds, weeks later. Ole Nadunguenkop tells Setek, "*Marafiki wako walitusaidia sana. Sasa tutapata mashamba.* Your friends really helped us. Now we will get land." Setek tells us that Ole Nadunguenkop will probably start looking for a market for that land on hearing that title deeds are coming.

Ole Nadunguenkop is the first living signpost we meet of an Ogiek schizophrenia that wavers between the Ogiek as conservationist and the

Ogiek as land broker. When it comes to the Mau Forest, he will not be the last. Like Samuel Kamikil/Salaton Ole Nadunguenkop, many Ogiek we eventually encounter seem to be two things, an interface between the ideal and the real: Samuel Kamikil, who claims to be dispossessed and landless, is a forest dweller and hunter-gatherer who lives on honey; and Salaton Ole Nadunguenkop, who is a Mau Forest broker, is a landowner, and drives a Subaru. After Kamikil/Ole Nadunguenkop we encounter the interface between Ndorobos, who in reinventing themselves as Ogieks became one of the last indigenous Kenyan peoples, long-suffering and landless, and, on the other hand, the members of large, rich Ogiek landowning families who are lawyers, professors, human rights activists, and NGO heads, and who are dabbling in eating forest. A protector, I suppose, is free to do anything with what he protects, and he is also free to claim an innocence at the same time.

Later in our travels in the region, we will acquire a 54 million Kenyan shilling sales agreement with Ole Nadunguenkop's name on it. A source reveals to us that Kamikil is probably just an agent for more powerful forces in Narok South involved in the large-scale illegal sale of the Mau South Forest. The names of powerful Narok politicians come up. In a sense our theory and observations about Ogiek schizophrenia are not necessarily true. And then I remember him telling us that he cannot read and write, and that he signs everything with his thumbprint. *Naweka alama*. But I also remember him saying that his father took him to school.

Look at the Killer!

EUPHRASE KEZILAHABI

TRANSLATED FROM THE SWAHILI
BY ANNMARIE DRURY

Yesterday I killed three words pitilessly.
The complex word I hit in the air;
it fell into pieces that can't be rejoined.
People should look for a new word now.
"Heaven" was gliding around in the clouds
surprised to see what had occurred.
I struck, it broke, and its life trickled away;
the word lay splattered on the ground.
"Death" I discovered dancing naked in the cemetery;
unceremoniously, I buried it.
No one called me a hero.
I put on my little rings of bells, set a feather on my head
and went to market sporting a bracelet of fur.
Behind me, dancers followed along
chanting
"Look at the killer!"

Christian Revivalist

EUPHRASE KEZILAHABI

TRANSLATED FROM THE SWAHILI
BY ANNMARIE DRURY

A lion is chasing us,
me and my wife.
We climb an elect tree.
It sways, and we start sliding.
We're falling down,
the lion a few steps away.
    (Silence)
Suddenly the lion collapses,
its mouth touching my foot,
blood oozing from its head.
    (Silence)
Then close beside me I see him,
gun in hand, smiling.
Whoever believes in me I will not make fall, he says.
    (Silence)
Hallelujah! Hallelujah! Hallelujah!
    (Song, clapping)

HALLELUJAH!

Lamentations of a Coconut Tree

MIA COUTO

TRANSLATED FROM THE PORTUGUESE
BY ERIC M. B. BECKER

It was an event that made the Nation's newspaper, official and authenticated. The buzz about the coconut groves of Inhambane was worthy of headlines and exultant columns. It all began when, seated along Inhambane's seaside drive, my friend Suleimane Inbraímo split the shell of a coconut. From inside the fruit didn't gush the usual sweet water, but blood. Exactruly: blood, certified and unmistakable blood. But that wasn't the only astonishment of the matter. From the fruit sprouted a human voice, in cries and lamentations. Suleimane took no half-dismeasures: his hands, agape, dropped the coconut and blotches of red splattered about. He stood there, confwoozy, buffuzzled, spent. The shock caused his soul to dissipate in low tide.

When I ran to help, he still was in the same position, head stooped to his chest. Remains of the incident had been removed, hands washed, amnesic. Only his voice still trembled as he related the episode to me. I distrusted. Doubt, we know, is the envy that impossible surprises haven't happened to us.

—Forgive me, Suleimane: a coconut that spoke, cried, and bled?

—I knew it: you weren't going to believe me.

—It's not not believing, brother. It's doubting.

—Go ahead and ask, among these folk around here, ask about what happened with these coconuts.

I filled my chest to let my patience breathe. Strange things, I'm already used to. I even have a taste for stumbling upon these inoccurrences. But this was not the moment. We should have left that place long before. Our work had ended the week before and we still awaited news of the boat that would transport us back to Maputo. Not that the place wouldn't allow us some minutes' rest. Inhambane is a city of Arab manners, unpressed to enter time. The tiny houses, obscurlear, sighed in the weariness of this eternal measuring of strength between the lime and the light. The narrow streets are good for courting; it appears that in them, no matter how much we walk, we never stray far from home.

I watch in the bay the feminine blue, this sea that makes no waves nor creates urgency. But my travel companion already has a flea in his ear. When I ask about the arrival of the next boat, Suleimane wobbles, one foot then the other, as prisoners do.

—Every day, "it has to come today."

The man spoke in imperfect certainty. Because in that very instant, as if issuing from his words, breezes began to swell. It squalled. First, the banana trees fanned. Gesticulant, the leaves swayed, obsolistless. We didn't think it important.

After all, only a risk of wind is needed to fan the fruitful plants. They should be called, in that case, the fanana trees. But soon after, other greenery begin to shake in an anxious dance. Suleimane begins with a stammer:

—This squall isn't going to allow any boat.

I sit still, ever so languid to show I have no opinion. I unwrap the little cakes I bought a short time ago from the old ladies at the market. A kid approaches. I think: here comes one more cryinbeggar. But no, the child stays beyond begging distance. My teeth are ready for the taste when the kid's eyes grow wide, a shout rising in his throat.

—Mister, don't eat that cake!

I stanch my teeth, mouth in dread of who-knows-what. The boy renews his sentence: I was not to salivate on the flat cake. Explain he knew not how, but his mother came forward in sudden arrival, upon beckoning from the child. The woman entered the scene with colossal heft, grasping a nimble sarong.

—The child is right, I'm sorry. These cakes were made with green coconut, were cooked with *lenho*.

Only then do I understand: they offended the local tradition that holds sacred the still-green coconut. Forbidden to harvest, forbidden to sell. The unripe fruit, *lenho* as it's called, is to be left amid the tranquil heights of the coconut trees. But now, with the war, there'd arrived outsiders, more believers in money than in the respect of commandments.

—Many-many are these dislocated who sell *lenho*. One of these days they'll even sell them to us.

But the sacred has its methods, legends know how to defend themselves. Varied and terrible curses weigh over he who harvests or sells the forbidden fruit. Those who buy it share in the fortune. The shell bleeding, voices crying, all this is *xicuembos*, hexes with which the forefathers punish the living.

—You don't believe it?

The vast woman interrogates me. It's not long before she'll reel off her own variations, applying the principle that for he who half-understands two words of explanation won't suffice. Even before she speaks, those present click their tongues in approval of what's going to be said. In the good country way, each one seconds the other. Exclamations of those who, saying nothing, agree with the unsaid. Only then does the woman unwrap her words:

—I'll tell you: my daughter bought a basket way over on the edges of town. She brought the basket all the way here on her head. When she tried to take the basket off, she couldn't. The thing looked like it was nailed down; we all used our might but it didn't budge. There was only one remedy: the girl returned to the market and gave the coconuts back to the man who sold them. You hear me? Lend me a little more ear, right this moment. Don't tell me you didn't hear the story of neighbor Jacinta? No? And I add, sir: this Jacinta put herself to grating the coconut and began to see the pulp never had an end. Instead of one pan, she filled dozens until fear bid her stop. She laid all that coconut on the ground and called the chickens to eat it. Then something happened I can't well relate: the little chicks were transformed into plants, wings into leaves, feet into trunks, beaks into flowers. All, successively, one by one.

Quieter than a seashell, I receive her reports. I didn't want a mis-dis-understanding. Suleimane himself drank with anguish these stories of common man, fanatically creduligious. Until we were gone, leaving that place for a no-star hotel. We shared the intention to chase sleep. After all, the boat would arrive the following day. Our return trip was paid for, we no longer had to think about the spirits of the coconut groves.

Bags and suitcases tottering on deck, motors abuzz: that's how, at long last, we made our way back to Maputo. My animated elbow brushes Suleimane's arm. Only then do I notice that, hidden amidst his clothes, he carries with him the cursed coconut. The same one he'd begun to split open. I marvel:

—What's this fruit for?

—It's to send to get analyzed there at the Hospital.

Before I could draw on some reasoning, he countered: that blood, who knows in what veins it frolicked? Who knows if it was diseased, or rather, disAIDSed? He went back to wrapping up the fruit with an affection only meant for a son. Then he broke off, rocking it with a lullaby. Perhaps it was this lullaby of Suleimane's, I could almost swear it, yet he seemed to hear a lament coming from the coconut, a crying from the earth, in the anguish of being woman.

Faces and Phases

ZANELE MUHOLI

"I arrived on the scene to find Disebo's half-naked and lifeless body surrounded by community members. The wire that was used to strangle her had punctured her skin and was still lodged inside her neck, while about 20 cm of hosepipe was inserted in her mouth, tied with a shoelace, and left with water running inside her body."
— *Assah Molapo,*
relative of Disebo Gift Makau,
a lesbian who was murdered in August 2014

Despite the fact that LGBTI individuals in South Africa have the right to same-sex marriage and freedom of expression as stipulated in our Constitution, members of the black lesbian community have been beaten, cursed, paralyzed, butchered, "curatively raped," and even murdered as the result of hate crimes. The photographic series *Faces and Phases,* of which this portfolio is a small representation, has been a lifelong project for us and features the brave survivors of these hate crimes. Standing firm and posing proudly, the women photographed here challenge fear and fight invisibility despite being abused by society.

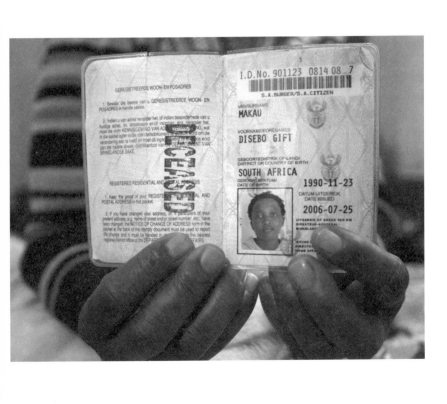

Ayanda Magoloza Kwanele
South Katlehong, Johannesburg, 2012

Bakhambile Skhosana
Natalspruit, 2010

Bathini Dambuza
Tembisa, Johannesburg, 2013

Musa Ngubane
Constitution Hill, Johannesburg, 2010

Xana Nyilenda
Newtown, Johannesburg, 2011

Sunday Francis Mdlankomo
Vosloorus, Johannesburg, 2011

Abomination

KEHINDE BADEMOSI

When Kehinde got off the bus in Lagos, he was weak from fasting but strong with the spirit of Sister Odolo, the Great Prophetess. The bus had dropped him off several blocks from his home on Market Street, where he lived with his twin sister, Taye, and his mother, Aduke, in a makeshift school. He had little more with him than a bag of Gala sausage rolls he'd bought along the way. It was after the New Year and most people had already left the city for the suburbs, where they celebrated the holiday with their families. Those who stayed had wrecked the city with parades and parties, leaving the streets littered with spent fireworks and the refuse of joyful celebrations.

Kehinde was eager to see Taye. He imagined that nothing dramatic had happened to her in the weeks he had been away. The doctors and psychiatrists had ensured that she would stabilize, but she still had occasional outbursts that were worrisome. Laura, his prayer partner from church, who had come to watch over Taye while he was gone, believed as Kehinde did that certain things were simply spiritual in nature, and only spiritual interventions could get rid of them. What afflicted Taye was a matter for prayer. Aduke was less certain, and her uncertainty tormented her. Was she to believe that her son, the newly anointed Preacher Boy, could bring home the miracle that would heal her daughter of her crippling psychosis? Or was she to have faith in the psychiatrist who claimed her daughter's illness was caused by a trauma of the "neural circuit"? No one knew exactly what that meant.

Laura believed in Kehinde. She was the one who knew Sister Odolo and had recommended that Kehinde visit her when the family's prayers for Taye went unanswered. Laura gave him comfort. Should anything happen at home while he was away, Laura knew how to reach him. People were always coming from and going to Ajebo campground for prayers, and if he was needed, all she had to do was send a note through one of the other believers.

It was easy to locate Kehinde at Ajebo campground. He was the scruffy Preacher Boy, the one who waited on Sister Odolo. Campers nicknamed him Elisha because they could call on him for special prayers whenever the Prophetess was unavailable. He learned quickly, and soon after arriving he was casting out demons. He had learned how to groan his prayers without actually speaking a word, a practice that was very peculiar to Sister Odolo. And as he groaned he would hold his stomach with both hands and writhe back and forth and left and right in a rhythmic fashion he couldn't control. And then all at once, he would cry out a cacophony of phrases that no one could understand. This style of prayer was called *birthing*. It was the prayer style of Sister Odolo that Kehinde had come to master. The indecipherable words he uttered startled sinners and made many confess their sins. Once, after Kehinde had led a session of prayer at Ajebo, a little girl confessed that during a meeting of witchcraft she had eaten two full-grown adults for dinner. Another man, visibly shaking under the influence of Kehinde's presence, related how he had been responsible for the misfortunes of his dying wife. When things got too heated during these revival meetings, Kehinde would call Sister Odolo to intervene. Whenever Sister Odolo arrived, there would be complete silence. Her eyes were sunk deep into large sockets on her oval face, and she didn't speak many words. Holding her stomach with her tiny hands, she would unleash a frenzied laughter that unsettled even the forest surrounding the campground. That was called laughing *in* the spirit. Kehinde had yet to master that when he left Ajebo.

Kehinde brought few possessions back from the camp. He had on the same plain gray shirt he had worn when he left Lagos. While at camp, he had washed the shirt and his underwear only twice, as Sister Odolo had barely given them time for such things. No serious gospel warrior would leave important activities like praying and fasting to wash their clothes. The Bible never recorded Jesus washing his clothes. Sister Odolo would say Jesus had no underwear to wash; all he had was a loincloth. *Seek ye first the Kingdom of God and all these things will be added unto thee.* Beauty. Grooming. Fashion. As far as Sister Odolo was concerned, these were frivolous activities that had led many believers to hell. In Kehinde's right hand was a big black King James Bible, rumpled at the edges, the pages packed with various bookmarks to get him quickly to the passages he needed.

The time was half-past eleven, and most vendors along Oke Alfa had closed their stalls. The dirt road was bumpy and potholed and littered with empty cartons of sugar and empty tomato tins flattened out by the passing trucks that delivered goods to the market. Walking the short distance home, Kehinde was hungry and feeling weak and feeble from fasting. He tore open the wrapped sausage rolls and sank his teeth into the cold bread and the beef buried within.

As he approached Oke Koto, the last bend before his home on Market Street, he felt a strong force pulling at him. He was now on a busy road, where the night market sold everything. The last time he walked that route was with Laura on their way back from the church. She had told him about the street and the sin-filled red brick building in the middle of all its busyness. She knew it well because she understood Hausa, the language spoken on Oke Koto.

The red building gave the street its life. People traveled from faraway states across Nigeria to trade there. They sold marijuana. They sold bets. They sold sex. The patrons of Oke Koto dressed piously to cover up the obvious nature of their trades, but Kehinde knew what was going on. Or he thought he knew. And what he thought he knew enraged him. He wanted to bring the Kingdom of God here. He needed to *birth* Oke Koto for God. He had been anointed by Sister Odolo, the Great Prophetess, to set the captives free, and Oke Koto might as well be the testing ground for his newly acquired spiritual authority.

Full of God's might, the Preacher Boy plunged into the crowd, making his way toward the red brick building. Outside the entrance, a *Mallam* grilled *suya* meat on the corner while a crowd of people waited in line for their orders. Kehinde entered the building, and the deeper he went, the dimmer it got. Faces were shades of dark gray, except for the occasional flicker of light from a cigarette lighter revealing hints of who they were. There were *Alhajis* in loose-fitting clothing negotiating in low tones with the prostitutes. Further in, he passed traders selling *Fura De Nunu* and *Zobo*, medicinal yogurts from Northern Nigeria men used to thicken their semen and enlarge the male organ. There were boys, too, barely 12 years old, selling cigarettes and weed rolled in old newspapers. The buyers were older men, sometimes in their thirties, sometimes in their seventies. These older men rarely wasted time. They would beckon the boy of their interest. They would price the weed in the rolled newspapers. They would pay, and then take the boy and disappear inside a locked room. When the boys returned, they were usually too tired to continue with their trade.

Kehinde's breath quickened. His body hummed as if it were in tune with what he was seeing, but his spirit felt violated. This enraged him. Sister Odolo had told him it was okay to be angry at sin. Holy anger, she called it. Careful that no one was watching him, he slowly lifted his hand above his head and groaned his prayers until he was seized by the cacophony of unknowable language. He moved further into the red building. The Preacher Boy had come to Oke Koto on a mission.

Deep inside the building, Kehinde arrived at a large open space packed and throbbing with people. He stared incredulously; his eyes danced around in wonderment. Prostitutes lined the corridors, smacking gum, blowing bubbles, smoking cigarettes and weed, and some other things he couldn't quite figure out. He felt light-headed.

A well-dressed lady in a full *hijab* smiled and flashed a golden tooth. He looked around, unsure if the smile was meant for him. She sashayed toward him. Laura had told him that the prostitutes in Oke Koto kept their bodies covered so as not to offend their Muslim patrons. The lady walking towards Kehinde had a pretty face and breasts that could not be contained or hidden by the *hijab*. They burst out in full rebellion. Without saying a word, she took the Preacher Boy by the hand and led him into her room, where she sat him on the floor on the only cushion. The air in the room was different—it smelled of lavender and citrus mixed with tobacco and weed.

"I am Aminat." She sat close to Kehinde. "What's your name, *Alhaji*?"

"Hussein." Kehinde gave the name his Muslim father called him before Kehinde went the way of the church.

"How much will you pay for two sweet ones?" Amina asked in a pleasant Hausa accent. Then she slowly opened her dress and released her breasts. She pulled Kehinde close and caressed his unkempt hair.

"JESUS!" Kehinde cried, holding his stomach with one hand and his Bible with the other. He had come to *birth* Oke Koto for the Kingdom of Christ and to set the captives free. More angry than startled, Aminat got up quickly, grabbed Kehinde by the arm and pulled him toward the door. That's when Isiaku entered. Isiaku was tall, with thick hair and the chest of a boxer. He whispered something in Aminat's ear, and she left the room.

"The devil is using you all." Kehinde pointed his Bible at Isiaku.

"Ba turenshi," Isiaku said in Hausa, revealing his gold tooth.

"So you can't speak even a little English?"

"Ba turenshi," Isiaku repeated as he got very close to Kehinde and caressed his head as Aminat had. Kehinde felt something. He felt it in his bones and across his skin as Isiaku ran his hand across Kehinde's worn shirt to feel his chest. Kehinde's dick stiffened. He didn't like the way he felt, but he didn't fight it. He told himself he would confirm what Laura had told him about the red building: that men came here to have sex with other men. These men, the *dandaodus*, as Laura called them in Hausa, had been a part of Hausa tradition until Muslims tried to suppress it. Some *dandaodus* behaved like women. They wore the local makeup and dresses and danced for other, more masculine men at their parties. During the day, they cooked for their men, who called them their wives. Isiaku was one of the masculine *dandaodus*. He was an abomination unto God.

Sister Odolo had said that homosexuality was one of the seven great abominations that would bring America to its knees and allow her to take control of the White House. Homosexuality, according to Sister Odolo, was God's way of giving people over to their reprobate minds because they refused to acknowledge and worship Him. Kehinde believed every word handed down from the Prophetess. Sister Odolo didn't say it was so; The Bible said it was so in the Book of Genesis. In the Book of Leviticus. In the Books of Timothy and Corinthians. And in the Book of Romans, where it was written: *Men abandoned the natural function of the woman and burned in their desire toward one another, men with men committing indecent acts and receiving in their own persons the due penalty of their error.*

However, something in his far past kept calling out to him. He had had a dream about it and remembered it now, with Isiaku before him.

When Kehinde was 12 years old, he had developed an indescribable fondness for his head teacher's son, Tunde Tuoyo. At 15, Tunde was the oldest boy in class, having repeated several grades due to his poor academic performance. Kehinde liked to stare at Tunde endlessly any time they got together after school. Soon enough, Tunde began to stare back—the same fixed stare during which nothing was said. Tunde clearly enjoyed Kehinde's staring. One day after school, Tunde pushed Kehinde up against the wall, nailing his hands to the wall with his strong palms. Kehinde didn't resist. He closed his eyes as Tunde came closer until their foreheads rubbed against each other, then their noses. They seemed to breathe each other, and then their mouths connected as if they were chewing each other.

The Touyos relocated to Dubai, and everything about that kiss was supposed to have relocated with them. But Kehinde remembered every detail of it. The helplessness of it. The smell of onions on Tunde's breath.

That night in Oke Koto, as Isiaku pulled Kehinde closer, Kehinde breathed him in the way he had Tunde. Blood rushed in his veins. Isiaku gently took Kehinde's Bible and threw it in the corner. With his thick Hausa fingers he traced the outline of Kehinde's nipples, now visible under his shirt. Then, slowly as the lantern in the room dimmed, Isiaku thrust his lips on Kehinde's. Kehinde did not stop him. Perhaps he did not want to stop him. Like a lamb led to the slaughterer, he gave himself willingly to Isiaku.

Isiaku's hand moved further down along Kehinde's chest, and down to his abdomen. When his hand reached Kehinde's waist, he began to unfasten his belt buckle. Instead of spurning the invasion, Kehinde silently prayed that a higher spiritual power would win the battle that raged within and keep Isiaku from going any further. He prayed that he would stop enjoying the intimacy. He prayed that his dick would soften, and that his nipples would behave themselves. He prayed that Isiaku would stop.

Isiaku opened the clasp of Kehinde's belt and started to lower his head. In one cry, in the style of Sister Adolo, Kehinde *birthed* the spiritual strength that stopped Isiaku. The Kingdom of God suffered violence and violence would take it by force. Kehinde ran from Isiaku. He ran with all his strength out the door, down the crowded corridor, and out into the open street. The cool night air hit him hard. He walked hurriedly, hiding his face from everyone passing by.

Market Street had a curfew. Vigilantes assigned to close the rusty gates would be there any minute now. Kehinde walked fast, breathing in and remembering Isiaku as he made his way home. It wasn't garlic. It wasn't onions either. What he tasted in the back of Isiaku's mouth lingered. Was it a weed concoction or a sedative of some sort? He recognized Isiaku's cologne though; he reeked of it. It was one of those locally brewed by the perfumers in the North. Its smell was too spicy and floral, and lacked the woody base of most imported colognes. Powerlessly, he carried the aroma all over his broken self the whole way home.

❀

It was Laura who opened the door for him, and he felt her gaze pierce through him as if she knew the smell of Isiaku's strong essence. Surely, Laura wouldn't think of Oke Koto. The Preacher Boy was just returning from Ajebo campground, and he must be coming with fire.

"I wasn't expecting you so late." She put her finger to her lips, gesturing to not disturb Taye, who was asleep.

Aduke's eyes were also shut, but Kehinde felt her gaze fixed upon him. Aduke never really slept. Even when she closed her eyes, she saw everything.

Kehinde hurried to the shower just behind the classroom and washed his body endlessly. He needed to get rid of Isiaku. He scrubbed. He pinched. He pulled at his skin. He added more Dettol to the water so the smell of the disinfectant would neutralize the odor, but the smell of Isiaku remained.

Sister Odolo would be saying her midnight prayers soon. The Great

Prophetess could see things, and he was sure she had seen him at Oke Koto. He knew she would divine it. She would divine the floral perfume. She would divine the taste of weed in his mouth, the semen in his underwear. She would divine it all. What about the church? What would the church do if they heard he had kissed Isiaku? He had been tempted and he had failed. He would be excommunicated.

The last Preacher Boy at Oniwaya had sinned against the church and gone the way of madness. No one could cheat Jesus. When He said, *Thou shall not fornicate*, He meant it wholeheartedly. Preachers serving at the altar must purify themselves, or the church could banish them for being unclean. He thought about his mother and the shame of Taye's mental illness. He thought about what had happened at Oke Koto and he became afraid. In a recent dream, he had been chased by thousands of swine. Ugly round swine chasing him and sniffing his ass with their snouts. They chased him down into a very deep valley, and when they caught up to him, they tore at his pants. They ate his leg while he watched, completely paralyzed by fear. They chewed and snorted, ripping at his flesh as they ate their way up his leg, past his knee, his thigh, his groin, and just as they were about to devour his male organ, he woke.

That night, he decided to sleep by the coconut tree, far away from the piercing eyes of Laura and Aduke. He was growing up too fast, and his body was trying to catch up with his spirit. He touched his underwear still wet with his own semen. He looked up at the coconut drupes; they reminded him of large balls, large eyes that belonged to Sister Odolo. They were all watching him.

He placed his hands on his stomach. *For we wrestle not against flesh and blood but principalities and power in heavenly places.* He needed to *birth* a miracle for himself now. He had been anointed the Preacher Boy, and his body must obey the Lord.

xxi

CLIFTON GACHAGUA

i cannot claim we invent any games, any more than they might say
we've been invented by the people who sit in the garden looking back
at us. passion. orange. guava. mango. zambarau. coming to the orchard
only after we are spent from hurting each other, tired from performing
and inventing ways of dying, we count fruits by a certain order: those
that promise to fall, those ripe only for worms, those cursed to bit-
terness. not knowing what to do with the unreachable, we throw stones
at them.

the canopy is so thick the place stays dark. we never see her. it is
understood she is there and we are never to be seen in the trees. she is
there in her blue garments, moving behind the trees, standing guard,
turning into plant, knitting time into the fur of cats. if a fruit falls it
belongs to the earth. sometimes she inspects a fallen fruit, always leaving it where it fell. so from an early age we learn to observe decay from
a distance, not sensing it in each other.

one day the lady comes out for a stroll. we hide behind a door, watching
her from the spaces between the loose wood. seventeen cats trail her,

none daring to walk past her, their heads beautiful in the sun—her children. they look at us and fling their shawls around their necks, strutting like newcomers at a festival. two cats lick her pale feet, their tongues hard and wet and pink, another wrestles with the tail of her blue garment. we follow her round the block, thinking if the hour is suitable for licking each other. we throw stones and exchange blood and mascara and artificial sweetener. latecomers. she stops for a while at the jacaranda tree and kisses it. four years we have pissed on that tree. I think the lesson here is forgiveness. or forgetfulness.

at night we watch her shadow in the orchard. you give me your eyes— evening light. we follow her movements, our legs wrapped in bandages. at the centre she sits stooped, her hands full of dirt, strangling cats, as one might wring a favorite cotton dress the night before church. she buries them under the flowers of the mango tree. you want to know why i always refuse to come on your belly.

we talk less and less, pay no attention to the whistling and tsk tsk tsk of the people in the garden. we learn how decay starts, how to sustain it, how to fear each other by loving animals, how to knead mud to get rid of all the air. mostly the beginnings of foreign alphabets.

xxviii

CLIFTON GACHAGUA

maybe we'll never know how this can
be—the yellow, the length. and what's lila?
you'll be tall all your life.
always mistaking love for (an) assassination.
and the halls—they will be there,
carpeted, busts, orange,
MK Abiola and war generals.
ways of dying—you'll be there,
listening, dreaming, in the way only
people like us can.
and by that i mean walking down Grogon,
a black river.
we will be all we can—listening
to the unnecessary, praising
bad men. and violence.

How the Son Wounded the Lion

RIBKA SIBHATU

TRANSLATED FROM THE FRENCH
BY ANDRÉ NAFFIS-SAHELY

Şïnṣïwai! "I have a story to tell!"
Uāddëkoi ṣẹlimai! "We're ready, we're listening!"

Once upon a time, when stones were made of ĥmbascā bread, a boy roamed the savannah all on his own because he had lost his parents.

A lion was also roaming the savannah, and because he was hungry, he was looking for prey. Eventually they crossed paths. Despite his hunger, the lion took pity on the boy and told him: "You'll stay with me until we find your parents. I'll protect you, just like a tree shelters us from the sun." Then he took the boy with him. The boy happily accepted the lion's offer and they started living together.

Time went by, and there was still no trace of the boy's parents, but by then the boy had become a young man. Having failed to find any trace of his parents, the lion had given up on his quest to reunite the boy with his family and had started to think of him as his own.

One day, the lion was napping atop a hill when two passersby arrived in the vicinity and sought shelter from the sun by sitting inside a cave. The two people were unaware that anyone else was around, so the lion was easily able to eavesdrop on their conversation. The lion eventually realised that they were the boy's parents; especially when they started talking about the child they'd lost, meaning the little boy whom he'd come to think of as his own. Now that he was certain, the lion decided to follow them in order to find out where they lived.

Having returned to his lair, he gave the boy the good news and took him to see them that very day. To celebrate their miraculous reunion, the boy's parents—whom, as it happens, were very wealthy—invited distant relatives from near and afar to attend a bountiful banquet. There was a great coming and going of people in their house for an entire week, and the trilling of women could be constantly heard. Every night, the lion would sneak back into the village to eavesdrop on the nice things people were saying about him.

However, one night the lion was greatly aggrieved and surprised to overhear what his adopted son had to say about him. On being asked by an old childhood friend, "How could you possibly sleep while in the sharp embraces of such a beast?" the boy had nastily replied: "I liked sleeping between his paws! It made me feel safe and loved. The only thing I couldn't stand was the stench of his armpits! Now *that* was truly terrible!"

As soon as he heard his son, the lion thought: "Poor me, it would have been better if I'd never heard that." He regretted having gone to the village and made his way back to his lair, sad and disheartened.

After some time had passed, the boy went back to his adoptive father, as had been agreed. Despite noticing the lion's gloomy expression, the boy thought this was just a case of jealousy, and so he told his adoptive father about all the exciting things he'd been up to that week, thanking him for all that he'd done for him during all those years.

After having listened to the boy in silence, the lion grabbed a spear and told his adopted son to pierce him in the chest with it. The boy refused to do such a thing, but the lion kept insisting and in the end he told him that it wasn't a request, but an order. The boy therefore relented, grabbed hold of the spear and stabbed his adoptive father, although he fell to the floor as soon as he'd done so, almost as though he'd been stabbed too. Once he regained consciousness, the boy lovingly tended to the lion's wound.

The wound healed after a few days, and only left a tiny scar in its wake. The lion then summoned his son and told him to go back to his real parents and never return.

"What? Why can't I ever come back? I can't leave you alone!" the boy told him, astonished.

"Yes, never," the lion replied. "Deep down, you must be happy that you're going back to your real parents; after all, *their* armpits don't stink! My son," he added, "some wounds can heal, like this one right here, where you see the scar, but there are other kinds of wounds, like the betrayal of a son, which can never heal, and they end up rotting the soul."

So the boy returned to his real parents and never saw his adoptive father again.

As for the lion, he left the savannah and went to live in a distant forest.

> *If you forget what you've heard,*
> *death will forget you in your turn,*
> *but if you keep on remembering,*
> *may God grant you all the corn you can eat.*

Whips

UNOMA AZUAH

This place felt like a prison. The bread and tea they gave us for breakfast was stale and weak and didn't seem to serve any purpose. I was hungry and came alive as soon as other students started gathering their notebooks, getting ready to dash out of class for lunch. All my excitements were usually short-lived. I had hoped that whatever we were having for lunch would be rice and stew. In the refectory, food was divided among the tables, so there were five to six students per table and each table had a pot of *garri* and soup. Sometimes, the soup was too watery, or the rice and beans had small pebbles. I had the responsibility of dividing up the food. Nobody appointed me but I volunteered as often as I wanted. Occasionally some students accused me of not doing a good job. At one point one of the girls at the table, Amaka, who had a large head, yelled at me, "Unoma, the fish on your plate is bigger than others."

"Bigger how?" I said. "I shared the fish equally."

"No, yours is bigger!" she yelled.

I shoved my plate to her and snatched hers, but she pulled it back, spilling some of the *Ogbono* soup. I clenched my fist and glared at her. I didn't want to get into trouble by fighting. Otherwise, I would have punched her big head. The rest of the girls at the table told me to calm down and to ignore her.

I got food for my school mother and brought it back to our dormitory, House Five. There was still a long line of containers in front of the water tank and that annoyed me. My containers had been in the line for hours. I was tired and ready for the afternoon rest, but there were about 15 containers ahead of mine. As I waited, I saw Nkechi sneek up to the water tank and look around to see if anyone was watching her. I looked down so she wouldn't notice that I had seen her. Then she pushed her blue container next to the second one in line.

"What do you think you're doing!" I cried.

Nkechi rolled her eyes at me. "Unoma Azuah, mind your business!"

"Take that container to the back of the line," I said, pointing at the trail of containers.

She hissed and started to walked away, leaving her container where it was, but I kicked it out of the queue. She picked it up and left.

A few minutes later, the lined moved and I pushed my container forward, glad to be moving ahead.

"Unoma Azuah! Unoma Azuah, your name is on the list!"

I didn't recognize the voice calling out my name. She had to be one of the new prefects. My heart pounded. A couple of weeks before, two girls had fought in House Four. When they were asked why they had fought, they said it was because of me. Even though I didn't ask them to fight over me, I was still told to cut the overgrown grass near the staff quarters.

I whispered a prayer and asked, "What list? Why is my name on the list?"

"You have a lover. You people have sex. Other girls are kneeling down in front of the principal's office. Go and join them."

There were about a dozen of us kneeling. The jagged stones ground into my knees and pierced my nerves. The sun's heat bore down with heavy hands. It was not long before the principal's whip snapped upon my back. I squealed in pain and begged for forgiveness. Instead, the principal punctuated every lash by saying, "Remember this pain when you commit your sinful act!"

After giving us all uncountable lashes, the principal strutted into her office in a huff. We were to kneel under the intense heat for another hour. When we were finally dismissed, I could still feel the pain breathing through the slashed surfaces of my back. I didn't want to feel the judgmental gaze of my bunkmates. I didn't want them to cast glances of *you deserve what you got*. So, I climbed the stairs to my classroom and cried. I was not in there for long before one of the *born again* girls came in with a Bible.

"Unoma, God loves the sinner but not the sin. I came to pray for you."

"I don't need your prayers," I said.

"So you're not ready to renounce your sin."

"Leave me alone!"

"The spirit of lesbianism is stubborn and demonic. I can start prayers and deliverance for you now, if you believe."

I looked at Ngozi as she talked about prayer and deliverance. Our eyes met. A chill crept down my spine. There was fire in her eyes, with sparks of madness. I moved away from her. I sat by the open window and gazed out. A couple of yellow birds chirruped and darted around the hibiscus flowers scattered around our classroom building. Their chirps drowned out the echoes of Ngozi's prayers as she slammed the Bible hard against her lap, casting out demons.

That's when I heard them, the hymns of the reverend sisters coming from the convent next to our school. The song was soothing but mournful at the same time, and it settled like a blanket of melancholy over my shoulders. That could be my place of refuge: the convent.

FICTION

The Garden of Tears

MOHAMED NEDALI

TRANSLATED FROM THE FRENCH
BY ANDRÉ NAFFIS-SAHELY

TRANSLATOR'S NOTE

Driss and Souad are in their late twenties and have recently gotten married. Driss is a nurse and Souad is a waitress at one of Marrakech's finest hotels. They work hard and are hoping to save enough money to buy their own home. During one of her evening shifts, Souad is assaulted by a drunken police commissioner. Outraged, the couple file a complaint with the authorities, and look on despairingly as both the police and the courts refuse to prosecute the commissioner. The novel is based on a true story and is a searing indictment of corruption and injustice in present-day Morocco.

Doctor Derkaoui showed up for his shift happy as a clam at high tide. He was smiling and humming a popular tune by the famous Southern Moroccan singer Oulad El Bouazzaou about getting drunk and having affairs. He shook my hand vigorously and gave me a friendly slap on the shoulder.

"All good, Driss?"

"No, Doctor, it isn't."

"Is it still about that matter to do with your wife?"

"Yes."

"How is the case coming along?"

"It's still in the magistrate's hands."

"More like stored in some dark recess!" he sneered.

"What do you mean by 'some dark recess,' Doctor?"

"That's where this country's judges stick tricky cases like your wife's!"

"And how long are they kept there, Doctor?"

"It depends, ten, fifteen, twenty years . . . and when the accused is a powerful government employee, just like in your wife's case, the trial is simply postponed indefinitely."

"If I've understood you well, Doctor, this means that government employees are never prosecuted in this country!"

"Only the small fry, but never the big fish, or almost never, that is."

"And why is that, Doctor?"

"One of my friends is a public prosecutor, and one day I asked him the same question. He told me that judges are under explicit orders that forbid them to formally prosecute any state employees and bring them to justice, no matter what the charges are."

"Why?"

"My friend told me this is so as not to compromise what they call the *hiba*, or the aura of untouchability that surrounds all of the state's high-ranking functionaries. His argument was the following: if the kingdom's courts ever prosecuted any authority figures, then the citizens would drag every state employee before the tribunal: police officers, traffic cops, prefects, governors, ministers; even the king himself wouldn't be spared!"

"So, you're telling me that in the name of this damn *hiba*, state employees can do what they like without ever being prosecuted?"

"Pretty much, and in the case of repeat offenders, the state itself intervenes and puts *internal sanctions* into effect. The worst that can happen to such a repeat offender is that they are forced into early retirement. This is how the state punishes its thuggish servants, by giving them a pension. Morocco truly is an amazing country!"

Before leaving, Doctor Derkaoui pulled a piece of paper, which had been folded in two, out of his shirt's breast pocket. He unfolded it and read it out in a mocking tone:

"The general management grants all hospital workers an hour and a half to carry out their duties as citizens . . . "

He left the piece of paper on his desk and left, humming the same popular tune as when he'd come in.

I had been in the midst of reflecting on what Doctor Derkaoui had said when a 50-year-old patient came to ask for my permission to leave the hospital.

"Where are you going, Moulay Ali?" I asked in a perfunctory manner.

"I want to carry out my duty as a citizen!" he replied.

"What duty are you referring to, Moulay Ali?"

"Why, I'm going to vote, of course!"

"You're free to go, Moulay Ali, but please don't come back too late, and above all, no cigarettes or alcohol!"

"Oh, that's all behind me!" he promised.

Each time he left the hospital, Moulay Ali came back drunk as a poet on payday. Sometimes, the police brought him back in their patrol car, after having extorted the last *dirhams* he had left in his pocket. Having reached the threshold of his office, Moulay Ali suddenly turned around and said:

"Tell me, Mr. Driss, are you going to vote as well?"

"Why do you ask?"

"Because the radio said that all the kingdom's employees have the right to an hour and a half to carry out their duty as citizens."

"In all honesty, I'm not sure I'm going to go."

"May I know why, Mr. Driss?" he asked with curiosity.

"Because . . . " I replied, doubtfully, "because . . . because I didn't get my voter registration card."

"Actually, they said on the radio that all citizens like you who didn't get their voter registration cards just have to go to the nearest polling station, present their IDs, and they'll be able to get their registration cards right there and then and thus carry out their duty as citizens on the spot!"

"If that's the case," I told him, in order to bring that boring conversation to an end, "I'll go and vote as well."

"You must, Mr. Driss! Especially since the polling stations will be open until seven o'clock this evening."

"I'll be sure to go, Moulay Ali! But you must get back here sooner than usual, and above all, don't forget to heed my advice!"

"Well, *I* certainly took your advice!" said Razane, who had just entered the office.

"You went to vote?" I asked.

She bent down and whispered in my ear:

"No, I got laid!"

"You . . . ?"

"Oh yes, I . . . "

"With who?"

"You know with who!"

"So how was it?"

"It reminded me of my first time with my husband! I think poor Doctor Derkaoui is madly in love with me!"

I'm not sure how to explain it, but when Razane confessed what she'd done, I experienced a great deal of admiration for her. It was as if she'd just accomplished something extraordinary: a feat of prowess, a brave exploit, an achievement.

Statement

EUPHRASE KEZILAHABI

TRANSLATED FROM THE SWAHILI
BY ANNMARIE DRURY

Morning.
I'm in a tourists' vehicle.
Here's what I saw:
a male lion chasing a zebra.
He leaps onto her back, catches her round the neck,
and she falls with a cry.
The lion starts to rend her belly,
his banquet a privilege of his strength.
Baboons hoot in the tree.
Beauty of the Creator's art
ravaged in a short while:
it's not a statement.

But
I remembered some news I read
on the city bus:
yesterday evening, a young man,
name undisclosed,

molested a girl of sixteen.
Tyranny of strength undoing
humane character in a short while—
and the punishment, light.
That's a statement.
It's still morning.

Being Here

EUPHRASE KEZILAHABI

TRANSLATED FROM THE SWAHILI
BY ANNMARIE DRURY

To tell you the truth, I got to be in heaven
looking around for a very short while
within the ideas in God's memory.
When he forgot me, I slid into a tiny opening
in the dance of surprise
and like a larva I swam
heroically in a river of tears
until I bumped against a soft wall
and entered inside to become a living creature.
There I rested in life's fertility.
When I recovered my strength
I struggled back into the river of tears.
I exited through a window and dropped down alive.
I saw for the first time
the wealth that had long hidden itself in me.
I cried with happiness.
Then I began to enjoy
the sweetness and rightness of being here.

When God remembered
and saw his example outside himself
he gave me a name and a number
and I played that game in which each day
thousands are taken off the field
never to return.

Therefore
I know one day he'll call me into his courtroom
where angels and devils wage their battles of advocacy.
I'll be tried for all I did in freedom
and for that bad poetry that caught his attention.

Petty Blood Sport

EFEMIA CHELA

He injured me is how we met. He kicked me in the shin in the line for free wine.

My little world {*Is this oaked?*

iPhone,

glass,

cigarette.

There are so many people here} jolted.

Suddenly my hands were empty and everything was cracked. Though it wasn't my fault, I said sorry. He was sorrier. My silk shirt was stained and blotchy and red like my cheeks when he brought me another glass.

"It's a thing. I'm sorry. It wasn't deliberate. I can't help it. It's a—"

We murmured late into the spring night about what made us both wrong. There was a lot. I write too many lists. I can only cry out of one eye. The left one is too sentimental and the right one too cold. We both understood trouble and what it was like to have half of you propelling forward and the other half yanking you meanly back. A constant gripping of the back of your neck. Or even worse, the imagining. The anticipation of it. The fear-in-waiting.

He kicked me again while we were goodbye-ing.

"I can't help it. Fuck. Shit. Cunt. Fuck. Sorry."

"Neither can I," I said, leaning in for a kiss, using his ear as a handle.

He said it was to be goodbye. I didn't know what that meant. For our petty blood sport to be over. No more bruises to pepper my pallid body. And no kisses to soothe them after. No one to tell me to quit smoking these joyless fags. Or to quash them when I fall asleep. I woke up one day and his side of the bed had burned. The sheets and pillow and most of the mattress. All from a lazy hand and a stealthily glowing butt. Fire had eaten it away. A friend of mine told me it was a sign to move on. Lucky I wasn't fucking dead, is what she said.

But I don't choose to keep Sam burning on. I love him like a reflex. Another in my list of bad habits. The only animate one. So animate people thought he was beating me, when he wasn't. I reach for him in my mind when I'm alone. In the gaps between things, meetings, and people, he waits. Beckoning, then dissipating. Leaving me full yet wretchedly empty. My memory is full but I am empty.

Filled with the scent of wild sage.

Wild sage crisping up is what Botswana felt like. When we drove through it, all dust and acacias and a heavy dry heat sifting into your throat filling you up until you thought you'd combust. We were road-tripping along and he wondered what smelled of sausage and mash? This black Englishman who should have known his colonies better. The sage surprised him. We stopped to pull up a bush. It wasn't too committed to its home. It shook loose easily. A stride or two and a few clods of dirt and we put it on the back seat.

"Should we water it before we go onto the pan?" I asked. Parked at the edge of a cracked mirror, the dried-up salt pans, I felt like we were on the final frontier. Together in the same space. Sam was so dark it was always a surprise to see his palms or soles. A flash of white lightning. As shocking as this other world. Coruscating, blinding, and alien.

We walked along it. Too dazzled to take photos. Just looking. Seeing. Absorbing. And letting our retinas be seared with the memory of salt.

When we got home we spent a lot of time at train stations. He saw me off to work. I hated sitting in traffic, and he could barely commit to the same vehicle for the whole holiday, let alone settle on a car to buy. The train was always too late or too early, like all the big events in life. Never on time and never fully wanted. It just zoomed up upon you. Too loud to ignore. It creaked like an old man during the rains. Then hordes of people bustled on and off. Frowning and sighing while being swallowed by this city beast. Whooshing through its entrails then being spat up somewhere else. It was a busy summer, wet and sunny. Humid, the days groped and fondled. They left their sweaty handshake on you.

Essentially, expensively, he couldn't sit still. Or work. He was the bull. The world an exclusive china shop. It was a condition. There were medications I would remind him to take. There were appointments he would choose to forget. It was worse when he was stressed, then he would buck and quake for minutes at a time. My graceful lover gone. His arms and legs the devil's playthings.

By autumn we were just alone together. There was never a right time to talk. He just sat, collar ripped and dangling, around his collarbone. He waited for the next forced puppet show and sat by all the things he'd accidentally punctured or broken, vibrating from the recent violence. I hesitated to clean them up. Not knowing when to move in. We were out of tape again. I felt like we were always running out of tape. And out of breath. I had to stop smoking so much.

We were waiting on the platform. My left eye (*disobedient thing*) cried as he broke up with me. I tapped my feet and wiped roughly at it to try and get it to stop. The left shoulder of my jacket was beginning to get moist. I hated the smell of wet felt. Time was frozen. It bit at my nose. I watched him lean into death. His last movement, one he meant.

He said it was to be goodbye.

UNOMA AZUAH is listed as one of the top English professors teaching at private colleges and universities in the United States. Her writing awards include a Hellman/Hammett grant, an Urban Spectrum award, the Leonard Trawick award, the Association of Nigerian Authors/NDDC Flora Nwapa Award for her debut novel *Sky-high Flames*, and the Aidoo-Snyder Book Award for her novel *Edible Bones*.

ROTIMI BABATUNDE was awarded the 2012 Caine Prize for African Writing for his story "Bombay's Republic." In 2015, he was longlisted for The Sunday Times EFG Short Story Award. His plays have been staged in several countries, including Sweden, the United Kingdom, and the United States. Babatunde is a recipient of fellowships from the MacDowell Colony, Ledig House, and the Bellagio Center. He lives in Ibadan, Nigeria.

KEHINDE BADEMOSI is a human factor design specialist with over 15 years of management experience in branding. In 2008, Bademosi founded Orange Academy, Africa's first practical school of integrated brand experience. Under the pen name "Kenny Brandmuse," Bademosi curates active online conversations about gay rights in Nigeria, where homosexuality carries a 14-year prison sentence under current laws. His first book and memoir, *The Exodus*, captures his life as a Pentecostal preacher boy who must cure his twin sister of a mental illness and overcome his taboo attraction to men.

Eric M. B. Becker is an award-winning translator, journalist, and writer. In 2014, he earned a PEN/Heim Translation Fund Grant for his translation of a collection of short stories from the Portuguese by Mozambican writer Mia Couto. He has also published translations of work by Brazilian writers Carlos Drummond de Andrade, Edival Lourenço, Paulo Scott, and Eric Nepomuceno. He is the editor of *Words Without Borders*.

Bree lives and works in Abuja, Nigeria.

Efemia Chela was born in Zambia in 1991, but grew up in England, Ghana, Botswana, and South Africa. She studied at Rhodes University, South Africa, and at Institut D'Etudes Politiques in Aix-en-Provence, France. When she grows up she would like to be a better writer and graphic novelist. She enjoys eating pizza, playing croquet, and watching black and white films. Her first published story, "Chicken," was nominated for the 2014 Caine Prize For African Writing.

Chimurenga *("Struggle for Freedom")* is a Pan-African project-based mutable object; a print magazine of culture, art, and politics; a workspace; and platform for editorial and curatorial activities based in Cape Town. Founded by editor Ntone Edjabe in 2002, it provides an innovative platform for free ideas and political reflection by Africans about Africa.

Mia Couto was born in Beira, Mozambique, in 1955. His novels and short story collections have been published in 20 languages. He was awarded the 2014 Neustadt International Prize for Literature and is one of ten finalists for the 2015 Man Booker International Prize. His work has been awarded major literary prizes in Mozambique, Portugal, Brazil, and Italy.

ANNMARIE DRURY is a poet and translator educated at Yale who studied with poets in Tanzania and Kenya, and at SOAS, University of London. In 2011, she received a PEN/Heim Translation Fund Grant. Many of her own poems have appeared in publications including *Raritan* and *The Paris Review*. She teaches at Queens College, CUNY, where she is a scholar of Victorian literature.

MARTIN EGBLEWOGBE is from Ghana. He is the author of the short story collection *Mr Happy and The Hammer of God & Other Stories* (Ayebia, 2012). He also co-edited the collection of poetry, *Look Where You Have Gone to Sit* (Woeli Publications, 2010). He is a co-founder and director of the Writers Project of Ghana. His story "The Gonjon Pin" appeared in the 2014 Caine Prize anthology.

CLIFTON GACHAGUA is the winner of the 2013 Sillerman First Book Prize for African Poets. He recently published a volume of poetry, *Madman at Kilifi* (University of Nebraska Press) and appears in a chapbook box set, *Seven New Generation African Poets* (University of Nebraska Press). He was recently selected for *Africa39*, a selection of the most promising 39 authors under the age of 40 from Sub-Saharan Africa and the diaspora. Clifton works at *Kwani?* as an editor.

BILLY KAHORA is the managing editor of Kwani Trust, where he has edited seven issues of *Kwani?* journal. His writing has appeared in *Chimurenga, McSweeney's, Granta Online, Internazionale, Vanity Fair,* and *Kwani?*. He is the author of the nonfiction book *The True Story of David Munyakei* and has been shortlisted for the Caine Prize twice. He wrote the screenplay for *Soul Boy* and co-wrote *Nairobi Half Life*. Kahora is also a contributing editor at the *Chimurenga Chronic*.

EUPHRASE KEZILAHABI is a major figure in Swahili literature, and the author of three volumes of poetry and six novels. Born in 1944 in Ukerewe, Tanzania (then Tanganyika), he came of age in the newly independent nation. Beginning with his first poetry collection in 1974, he has been centrally responsible for introducing free verse into Swahili. He is a professor in the Department of African Languages and Literature at the University of Botswana.

ZANELE MUHOLI was born in Umlazi township in Durban, South Africa, and lives in Johannesburg. She co-founded the Forum for the Empowerment of Women (FEW) in 2002, and in 2009 founded Inkanyiso, a forum for queer and visual (activist) media. Muholi's self-proclaimed mission is "to re-write a black queer and trans visual history of South Africa for the world to know of our resistance and existence at the height of hate crimes in South Africa and beyond." She has been shortlisted for the 2015 Deutsche Börse Photography Prize for her publication *Faces and Phases: 2006–14* (Steidl, 2014).

ANDRÉ NAFFIS-SAHELY's poetry has been featured in *The Best British Poetry 2014* and the *Oxford Poets Anthology* (Carcanet, 2013). Recent translations include *The Physiology of the Employee* by Honoré de Balzac (Wakefield Press, 2014), *The Selected Poems of Abdellatif Laâbi* (Carcanet, 2015), which won a PEN Translates! Grant from English PEN, and *Money* by Émile Zola (Alma Classics, 2016).

MOHAMED NEDALI was born in Tahanaout, near Marrakech, in 1962 into a family of poor farmers. Educated in Marrakech and at Nancy 2 University, France, he has taught at his local high school since 1985. He is the author of six novels. His debut, *Morceaux de choix: les amours d'un apprenti boucher (Prime Cuts: The Life & Loves of an Apprentice Butcher)* was selected by J.M.G. Le Clézio as the winner of the 2005 Grand Atlas

Prize, and for the International Prize of the Novel of Diversity at the Festival of Cartagena in 2009. In 2012, his latest novel *Triste Jeunesse (Sad Youth)* won the third La Mamounia Literary Award. *Prime Cuts: The Life & Loves of an Apprentice Butcher*, translated by André Naffis-Sahely, will be published by Ohio University Press in 2016. It was awarded a Hemingway Grant by the French Embassy in the United States.

RIBKA SIBHATU is an Eritrean poet who writes in Tigrinya and Italian. Born in Asmara in 1962, she was imprisoned for a year in 1979 due to her political activism and fled the country in 1980, moving first to France and then to Italy. Her publications include *Aulò! Bardic Poems from Eritrea* (Sinnos, 2009) and *The Exact Number of Stars and Other Eritrean Fables* (Sinnos, 2012). She was selected to represent Eritrea at the Poetry Parnassus held in conjunction with the London Olympics in 2012. Her poems were then translated and anthologized in *The World Record* (Bloodaxe Books, 2012).

ACKNOWLEDGMENTS

Different versions of "Normal," "Abomination," and "Whips" will appear in *Selected Stories from the Blessed Body*, a nonfiction anthology edited by Unoma Azuah.

"How to Eat a Forest: In Two Acts" is part of a longer essay titled "How to Eat a Forest," which was first published in April 2015 in *The Chimurenga Chronic.*

"Look at the Killer," "Christian Revivalist," "Statement," and "Being Here" are from the forthcoming *Stray Truths: Selected Poems of Euphrase Kezilahabi*, edited and translated by Annmarie Drury (Michigan State University Press, fall 2015).

Zanele Muholi's portfolio is from *Faces and Phases: 2006–14* (Steidl, 2014).

Passages: Africa
Contemporary Writing from the Continent

PEN
AMERICA
free expression.
literature.

PEN AMERICAN CENTER
588 BROADWAY, SUITE 303
NEW YORK, NY 10012
PEN.ORG

This series is made possible with generous funding from
FJC, A Foundation of Philanthropic Funds.

Opinions expressed are those of the author and artist of each piece,
and not necessarily those of the editors or the officers of
PEN American Center.

PRINTED IN THE UNITED STATES BY COLONIAL PRINTING
DESIGN BY SAM POTTS
COVER ARTWORK © ZANELE MUHOLI
ISBN: 978-0-9963008-0-3